CW01090893

THE
HITCHHIKER'S
HANDBOOK

by James MacLaren

Loompanics Unlimited
Port Townsend, Washington

This book is sold for information purposes only. Neither the author nor the publisher will be held accountable for the use or misuse of the information contained in this book.

The Hitchhiker's Handbook
© 1995 by James MacLaren

Published by:
Loompanics Unlimited
PO Box 1197
Port Townsend, WA 98368
Loompanics Unlimited is a division of Loompanics Enterprises, Inc.

Cover design by David Collier
Photo by Barbara MacLaren

ISBN 1-55950-125-1
Library of Congress Card Catalog 95-75679

Contents

Part One:
Miscellaneous
Introductory Shit

If I didn't like you I wouldn't fuck with you.

Who This Book Is For
And Who It's Not For

This book is written for anybody who might find themselves out there on the side of the road somewhere without a car, miles from where they want to be.

Whether by choice or not.

Mostly it's for the ones out there by choice though, because the ones who get stuck by accident probably disapprove of hitchhiking and hitchhikers and they're not gonna buy this stupid book anyway. But they should read it too or else they're probably never gonna make it when their time comes (and it's definitely coming).

There's a bit more to hitchhiking than just standing there with your thumb out. Quite a bit, actually. If you plan on doing it regularly like I do, then this is definitely the book for you. This also might be the book for you if all you want is to simply understand what it is that those guys are doing out there on the side of the road. The ones who do it all the time and have gotten good at it have a whole routine they go through. This'll tell you about that routine and why they do it.

This book AIN'T for you if you've got thin skin. Or can't take a joke. Or can't tolerate profanity. Or are some kind of humorless gay-rights activist or something like that. I'm gonna write for the majority. The kind of just plain folks I've known all my life. Go write your own damn book if you don't like this one.

4

Back to everybody else. The basic premise of this book is that you're actually gonna be doing some hitchhiking, and since most hitchhikers fall into a sorta group, I'm gonna aim this in the general direction of the sorta group. Folks that aren't too damn concerned with what everybody else thinks about 'em. Guys who aren't afraid to go out and do something a little different. Folks that can take a joke. Real people. (No snobs or high-falutin' posers allowed.) People who actually use curse words, drink beer, wear T-shirts, and even fart occasionally.

In public.

Got it?

So let's go.

Why Hitchhike

Why hitchhike? Why the hell not? It's fun. And this little piece of the book is gonna cover just that. Reasons for hitchhiking 'cause you want to.

There're a zillion reasons for wanting to stand out on the side of a road trying to get some total stranger to stop their car and let you in so as they can roll you across the countryside for free.

But mostly it's 'cause you either need to be somewhere and don't have the wheels to get there (whether by choice or not) on your own, or just for the sheer hell of it.

To start with, hitchhiking is free. Don't cost a nickel. Nuthin.' That's a pretty good reason right there. I mean, how else can you go from California to Florida in less than a week for nothing more than it costs to eat (and maybe, just maybe, sleep)? As long as you got the time, why not?

And don't go giving me that line about how dangerous it is. You're probably safer out there on the road than you are at home. There's more wackos creeping around on the streets of your neighborhood on foot looking for a house to break into right now than there are wackos driving up and down the street in front of the damn house.

Get serious.

Sure, people sometimes get it in the neck while they're hitchhiking, but think how many are getting it in the neck every day just sitting there watching *A Current Affair* or something equally dorfy on their TV. Yeah. So unless you've got plans to dig some kinda hole and live in it and never come outside where it's dangerous, don't give me any shit about how dangerous hitchhiking is.

Besides, some little old lady'd probably drive her Cadillac off the pavement and in on top of your head while you're sitting there in your stupid hole anyway.

Don't trust me? Fine. Go look up the mortality rates in the *Statistical Abstracts* or something. It's in your library gathering dust even as you read. The government prints stuff like that. So do the insurance companies. Go find out how many people die each year from really lethal goings-on like... flying in airplanes... getting stung by bees... falling off the step ladder... walking across the street... hit by lightning... going for a boat ride, and other countless gruesome delights.

EVERY separate one of those items kills and maims more people than hitchhiking every year.

When's the last time you heard the Mayor making an indignant speech calling for a ban on all boats? Or criminalizing step ladders?

In fact, I bet you'll have trouble just FINDING the numbers on hitchhiking. Know why they're hard to come across? It's 'cause the number of people getting killed or injured hitchhiking each year is so goddamned TINY! So forget what your mom told you about hitchhiking all those years. Your mom didn't know what the hell she was talking about.

Back to free. When you start to add up all the expenses of owning a car, you get pretty queasy.

First, you've gotta buy the damn thing. Then you've gotta fill it up with gas all the time. Plus, the state's gonna make you buy insurance for it, not to mention license tags and traffic tickets. Then stuff starts falling off it and you've gotta either buy parts and fix it yourself or, worse, have some greaseball ripoff mechanic charge you an arm, leg and one testicle to get it running again. And then you're gonna go and do something REALLY stupid like spend a grand on one of those loathsome super-stereo systems or something. And... well, you get the idea.

Cars are really fucking expensive. The wonder is that as many people own the damn things as do.

It wasn't 'till I got a REAL job (no, not writing books) that I shelled out the bucks for a car.

I suppose that if you're one of those jerks who really believes that ANYBODY (never mind those sexy blondes they're all the time showing in the commercials) actually gives a shit about what you're driving, then you can quit reading this.

There's no hope for you anyway and I don't really care if you read my book or not, 'cause you're a complete asshole.

You know the kind of creeps I'm talking about?

The bald-headed guy with his three strands of hair combed all the way across his head like it's gonna make me think he ain't bald or something? The one who's driving a little red convertible go-fast car and's got one of those dippy-looking driving caps on with a pipe in his mouth?

Or maybe the semi-retarded 19-year-old who's got a rich (but seriously stupid) daddy. Whamming around town in that goddamned Trans-Am or whatever the hell it is with the stereo cranked up to deaf.

Or even that bleached blonde with all the makeup on who's driving that Corvette. Doing thirty in the fifty-five zone. 'Till you try to pass her.

Those people are seriously fucked up. And they're never ever gonna be caught without some kind of machine wrapped around 'em to prop up their sagging egos. They have no use for this book. Come to think of it, I don't want to see 'em out on the side of the road with me either.

So anyhow, when you start adding up all the negative cash flow that's involved with having a car, you just might decide that it ain't worth it and go hitchhiking instead.

That's what I did.

For years.

Still do.

And it's really a breath of fresh air when you dump the gas guzzler. Really liberates you. You start looking at the way you get around town in a whole new light. Turns out that 80 percent of all those trips that were so important weren't. Same thing with HAVING to be here or there. Most of it's a lotta crap. Not required. Of course, if you want to hang around with the kind of people who are actually gonna think more of you 'cause of the manly car you drive, then go ahead. Ain't my problem.

OK. We've decided that we don't need the car anymore. Now let's look at some of the other things that you can accomplish by hitchhiking. They count as reasons for hitchhiking too, don't they?

How 'bout, for instance, commuting to and from work? Yep. Work. Work, as in gotta be there at 8:00 a.m. or they're gonna fire you. I did it myself for several years, so don't try to lay any shit on me about how it can't be done.

Or maybe just visiting friends. And that includes staying 'till the party is all the way over at 2:00 a.m. and then thumbing 30 miles back home. Did that too. Lotsa times. Don't want to get the idea that hitchhiking's limited to daytime or anything like that.

Long-distance travel is a good one. I mean really long. Like from coast to coast (and not just Tampa to Daytona Beach either). Done that too, needless to say. Visiting relatives is OK too. For a day or a week. Doesn't matter. Long as they've invited you first, though.

Hitchhiking to the ball game or rock concert is kinda neat.

And it's OK to put the old surfboard under your arm and head out from Kailua to Sunset Beach, too.

Is the picture starting to become clear? Whatever you can do with a car, you can do hitchhiking. Plus a lot of other stuff too.

Some of the cars I've owned wouldn't make it across the county, but my thumb was good for across the country.

Still is.

All for free.

The other big reason for hitchhiking is just for the hell of it. A killtime. A way to meet interesting people (the dull drab types don't seem to stop and pick you up much).

Or maybe go to some place you've never been before. For no good reason at all.

Just go.

There's nothing quite like having one of those warm lazy summer days with nothing to do and just hitting the road. Bang, I'm outta here. And standing there on the roadside with all the time in the world to go... where?

Who cares!

Pick a little dinky road out in the country with hardly any traffic on it at all. Where's the guy who picked you up going? Sounds good, I'll go there too.

Why not?

Good for cleaning the cobwebs outta your brain. Lotsa time for your mind to wander. Think about stuff. Any old thing that crosses your mind.

And the breeze is blowing and the birds are singing and there's neat puffy white clouds up in the sky... and you've got time for all of it. Nobody's gonna give you a hard time. Hell, nobody even knows where you are.

You're free.

Just standing there with your thumb out.

Daydreaming.

One of the other big reasons for hitchhiking is 'cause you gotta. It's the one that nobody wants to think about. Nobody wants to believe that some day their trusty iron steed is gonna poop out and strand them in the middle of nowhere. Or worse, a somewhere that's worse than nowhere. Like the very worst part of town. You know, where even the crack dealers are afraid to go.

Time for a reality check. When old reliable DOES leave you in the lurch, it's gonna be smack in the middle of one of those terrible places that you don't want to drive through even if you're a cop in a cop car. Or so many miles from anything that you wish you WERE in the middle of crackville. Or just maybe old Betsy decides to conk out in the middle of a hurricane or something. And you didn't think that Tennessee HAD hurricanes, didja? For things like this, you're gonna need help getting home.

All of the above being the case (and it is DEFINITELY a case of when, not if), it behooves you to know at least a little something about hitchhiking when the time comes. Your skill at getting a ride just might get you outta there before the bad guys discover you. Or the flood hits.

Another, peculiar, reason for hitchhiking is invisible travel. If you have some need to get somewhere without leaving the slightest trace, hitchhiking is the way to go. The extent to which you let people, cops and such-like know your true identity when you're on the road, is the extent to which you become visible while traveling. Excepting your physical description, you can write your own ticket when it comes to identification. Keep in mind, of course, that you MUST stay legal just the way the rest of this book tells you how to. As long as the cops have no SERIOUS reason to hold on to you and maybe fingerprint you, they can check you out in every state you visit without your true identity being revealed. It's your decision.

This, of course, brings us back to the purpose of this book.

Whether you know it or not, this book likes you. And it's very likely going to be what gets you out of the mess you're in, out on the lonesome roadside. This book's gonna help you even if you don't like me, hitchhikers, hitchhiking books or nuthin'. It doesn't care. It has a very nice attitude about things like that with one exception.

It has no feelings at all for people who don't read it. You don't read it, it don't help you.

So sue it already.

For being selfish.

What's Owed You?

Now that we understand why we're out there on the side of the road, perhaps we oughta consider what all those people whooshing by in their chrome capsules owe us. It might keep us from developing a bad attitude over things we're not getting that we think we're due.

In a word, those folks slamming down the road owe us one thing.

NOTHING.

Nada, zilch, zip, nuthin'.

Without a firm grip on this particular truth, hitchhiking ain't gonna be a whole lotta fun. You are inevitably going to be let down one day when you're in a hurry to get somewhere (which you have NO business doing whilst hitchhiking) and every last one of them bastards goes by at warp 8 without so much as a glance in your direction. This is surely going to befall you sooner or later and you must surely have it within yourself to keep from developing a shitty attitude as a result.

12

Otherwise, you're gonna have a look on your face. And as you will see later, that's bad. At least as far as getting a ride goes.

Conversely, if you expect nothing from that great raft of drivers going by you without stopping, whatever kindnesses that are given you will be seen for what they really are. A complete bonus.

Something for nothing.

What could be better than that? Your smile won't fade, and through some mysterious process that I do not understand, you will get rides quicker.

If you don't believe it, then take the trouble to time your rides when pissed and again when you're cheerful.

I did.

It works.

Go figure.

Part Two:
The Nuts And Bolts
Of Hitchhiking

So OK, let's go hitchhiking already. Enough Bullshit.

Picking A Good Spot

I suppose that to start out with when you're hitchhiking, the first thing you do is to walk over to the road and THEN start thumbing. Although you may not have noticed it, there's a decision that has to get made before you can even go stand by the road.

You gotta decide on a spot where you're gonna hitchhike.

So that's where we'll start too. Picking a spot. OK?

When choosing somewhere to stand, you gotta keep in mind what it's gonna be like for the guy who's whamming down the road in your direction at 60 mph. Here he comes driving like hell and not thinking about you or the fact you need a ride, when all of a sudden he looks up and there you are with your thumb out. He's only got a second or two to decide to stop, and anything that might give him second thoughts about stopping is gonna put him somewhere way down the road past you before he makes up his mind to stop.

Just about nobody stops and turns around to come back and pick you up once they're past you.

Things that keep people from pulling over include curbs, cliffs, cops, parked cars, signs, buildings and stuff like that. Safety hazards.

Just imagine yourself trying to stop for some dope who's thumbing on a blind curve with no road shoulder on an expressway. You'd have to be on some really strong stuff to decide to stop in a place like that.

Do you want to get a ride with a driver who's stupid enough to have to slam his brakes and block an onrushing wall of traffic just to give a total stranger a ride?

So before you turn around to face the traffic, do a little surveying of your surroundings and go stand in that perfect spot.

Like that one right over there.

What you're looking for is something like this: a very lightly-used turn or merge lane that runs on in front of and behind where you will be standing for a couple of hundred feet with no curb or drop-off to get in the way of people pulling ALL THE WAY OFF of the road. The area off the road wants to be a nice smooth shoulder (grass is nice but any solid level surface will do). All of THAT wants to be somewhere down towards the end of a long straight stretch of road that's got a low speed limit where drivers can plainly see you coming from way the hell off.

This best of all possible set-ups gives the driver plenty of space to slow down easily without some asshole on his butt laying mightily on the horn. And if by chance somebody decides to pull into that mostly unused turn/merge lane when your ride comes to a halt, no problem. Your ride just eases completely off the pavement onto that nice smooth area without so much as a bump.

Safety.

That's the ideal and of course you don't get it all that much. But if you keep in mind the fact that people need plenty of distance/time to check you over and then decide to pick you up in the first place, and then plenty of space in which to slow down, and then still more space over to the side of the traffic lane to keep them from getting slammed by the next idiot zooming down the road once they're stopped, and yet even more space to build up speed before they merge back into traffic, you'll soon become a real expert on picking a spot intelligently.

Go ahead and walk the extra distance it takes to get to that piece of prime hitchhiking real estate. It's worth it.

Another good spot is an intersection. But not just any old intersection. Since there're zillions of 'em (intersections, that is) out there, picking a good one shouldn't be too difficult. We'll do intersections in a lot more detail in just a moment.

That's all there is to it. Is that easy enough? Long straightaways with good access to a smooth shoulder and intersections. Just two places.

Now, of course, sometimes you're gonna get dumped out somewhere that won't fit the bill. No biggie. You'll still get a ride soon enough, but you gotta understand it'll take a little longer.

When you get right down to it, about the only two places to NEVER hitchhike are where there's a flood of cars zooming by without anyplace for somebody who's stopping to give you a lift to pull off the road all the way, or a spot just around a blind corner. Somebody'll stop alright, but it won't be much fun to watch 'em get rear-ended into the next time zone. And if you're half way inside the car that stopped when he gets it in the ass, well... you can forget making it to where you were going.

And probably a whole lotta other stuff too.

Intersections

OK, now let's do intersections.

If you're hitchhiking in town or even just a moderately built-up area, you're gonna have to come to terms with intersections.

The rules of hitchhiking intersections are real easy. There're just two of 'em:

1. Stay downstream of them.
2. Don't go too far downstream of them.

Is that easy enough to remember?

God, I hope so, or otherwise you probably shouldn't be out on the streets by yourself.

I'll elaborate a little so you can understand what's going on.

Before we go any farther here, gang, we better understand the directions I'm gonna be using here. And for the rest of the book too. YOU probably already know what I'm about to say, but for the benefit of anybody who might have the teeniest doubt about directions, here goes:

Up, or upstream ALWAYS means "in the direction the traffic is coming from." Just like with a river. Down, or downstream ALWAYS means, you guessed it, "in the direction the traffic is going towards."

Front, or in front of you, ALWAYS means the direction you should be facing when thumbing. Front and upstream are the same direction. Back, or behind you, ALWAYS means the direction to your rear when you are facing into the oncoming traffic when thumbing. Back and downstream are also the same direction. ALWAYS. Even when you're turned around the wrong way.

Outside means off to the side of the roadway. The road shoulders are outside the traffic lane. The smooth place for people to stop on so they can let you into their cars is outside the traffic lane. ALWAYS. Sometimes the area outside the traffic lane is still part of the pavement. Be careful when you're outside the traffic lane but still on the pavement. ALWAYS.

Now, back to the two rules of intersections.

For rule #1, it's pretty easy to understand that of all those folks going past you, a fair amount of them aren't going any further down the road beyond your present location than that next intersection back there behind you. Needless to say, all of THEM guys you can definitely ignore for the purposes of arriving at your destination whether they pick you up or not (yes, I've had people "help me out" with rides of a block or two).

Now, if that's not enough, there're also a whole bunch of cars pulling into traffic with people just looking for the next hitchhiker to pick up that can't stop for you 'cause there you sit like a dummy 200 feet upstream into all that oncoming traffic.

For rule #2, it's not much more complicated. When people are speeding along at 85, getting the damn car stopped is a teensy bit more of a bother than when they're doing... oh, say about 5.

Physicists tell us that while an object (a car for instance?) is undergoing acceleration its speed keeps increasing as long as it's accelerating (seems reasonable). So while that friendly Volkswagen that has just pulled into traffic from the intersection right in front of you is sputtering along towards you, it hasn't yet had time to accelerate and get going real fast.

And since people tend to do easier things more often than hard things (like stopping a car doing 85 in less than 50 feet), that slow-moving VW that pulled out right there in front of you is much more likely to stop for you than that hateful Porsche which has been accelerating at an unsafe rate continuously since cutting into traffic way the hell up there.

The slower the car's going, the more likely it is to stop.

Try to get as close to the corner as you can while maintaining all the little safety tidbits (like allowing for a place for the guy that stops for you to pull into that's off the roadway where nobody's gonna rear-end the shit out of him).

Right over there next to that long break in the curb where people can pull into the parking lot of the gas station looks pretty good to me.

There's one major exception to staying downstream of intersections (you just knew there would be) and that's when you're standing in the middle of town on a busy street with absolutely NOWHERE for anybody (even motorbikers) to pull over out of the way of the surging flood of oncoming traffic.

For that, you place yourself just in front of the intersection right even with the stop line. That's that thicker white line next to the two other white lines that define the pedestrian crosswalk (I betcha never knew what the hell that was there for did you?).

That's where the cars have to stop for the red light. Or at least everybody except that idiot who's got the front end of his Mercedes halfway out into the intersection just as if it's gonna get him home to his bimbo wife and drug addict kids any sooner than everybody else.

Once they're stopped, you put on your most pleading face (make sure it's a good one, 'cause they're all RIGHT THERE and not moving, so they can really get a good look at you) and make definite eye contact with each one of them in sequence starting with the guy at the head of the line right there next to you.

Don't break eye contact 'till you get a definite signal from the driver that you don't have a snowball's chance in hell of getting a ride with him or her (you'll know). It's times like this that paying attention to your appearance can really pay off.

You'd be surprised at just how successful standing at the traffic light can really be.

All that notwithstanding, this little ploy ain't worth a shit when there's a dedicated (you know, like devoted entirely to) right turn lane at the intersection you're standing by. The people in that lane are ALL turning right and aren't gonna do you a lick of good. The people in the next lane over who're gonna go straight are insulated from you by all those cars in the right-turn-only lane and can pretend they don't even see you.

Mind where you're at, OK?

Expressways

You can basically forget all that other stuff I just told you about where to stand when you have to travel an expressway to get to where you're going.

In general, expressways suck.

At first glance, it seems that an expressway oughtta be an ideal place to thumb a ride. I mean, look at the set up. It's perfect. Plenty of room on that shoulder lane for people to safely stop in, nice straightaways for good long-distance visibility, bunches of cars going by, lotsa streetlights for good visibility at night, the whole enchilada.

However, reality (Don't you just hate reality?) intrudes. For reasons that don't entirely make sense to me, people just don't stop for you on an expressway. I dunno, maybe it's 'cause they're all zooming by at warp 8 or something. Not only that, but with all those on- and off-ramps, mega-interchange cloverleafs and stuff like that, it gets a little dicey as to figuring out which way folks are really headed; and of course if you can't figure out where they're headed, then they ain't gonna do any better figuring out where the hell you're going either.

If they don't know where you're going, they're gonna assume you're headed somewhere else than they are and won't stop for you.

And on top of all that, there's the cops.

For grave reasons of public safety (which never in my life have I been able to quite fathom), the cops don't have much of a sense of humor when it comes to people like you and me hitchhiking on their fucked-up expressway.

So to hell with their stupid expressway, let's go over yonder to that on-ramp and hitchhike there instead. Rule #1 of thumbing on the expressway is: Don't thumb on the expressway.

That immediately brings up one of the things about hitchhiking on expressways that's no fun. You gotta walk your damn legs off to get way the hell and gone over yonder somewhere so as you can work the traffic from an on-ramp.

A little side note here. If you're unfortunate enough to be dropped off in the middle of one of those 10 square mile interchanges where everything's an expressway all the way to the horizon in every direction, give up and just go ahead and try your luck as is. Just try to find an arterial that feeds into the main route you want to take. That way, with people just entering the damn thing, there's a better chance that they'll stay on it for a while and maybe take you all the way out of that congested mish-mash. Good luck.

Back to the on-ramp. Finding and properly utilizing the on-ramps is about 90 percent of expressway hitchhiking technique.

Really.

There are two basic on-ramp set-ups.

Downtown (hopefully never), and out of the urban jungle on the Interstate (or something similar) in an open-type area.

We'll do the open area first, 'cause it's so much better to be on. Take note of the lay-out of whatever kind of set-up I'm describing. Hopefully that'll get you in the habit of taking stock of the local lay of the land when you're out on the road. You should be able to identify the lay-out of the ramp you're on at any given time.

In an open-type (not downtown) area, the on-ramp, or entrance ramp if you prefer, to the expressway is generally an extension of an ordinary road that had traffic lights and such. After the last light, or stop sign, it sorta heads off in the same direction as the expressway and then just kinda blends into it.

Get the idea?

I hope so, 'cause that ramp's got two ends (the one end at the plain old normal road and the other end at the expressway) and we're gonna deal with both of 'em.

Which end you want to work usually depends on the traffic density. The heavier the traffic, the more you oughtta be inclined to use the upstream end of the ramp that connects to the normal type road. Remember, you want to stay off the main part of that lousy no-good rotten expressway every chance you get.

A major exception to this strategy comes when there is nowhere on the ramp for people to safely pull over out of the way of oncoming traffic to pick you up. When faced with something like that, go on and walk down the ramp 'till you get to someplace where people can get all the way outside the traffic lanes to stop and pick you up, keeping the thought in mind that the farther down the ramp you go, the faster everybody's driving and the faster everybody's driving, the less they'll be inclined to stop their car for you.

So OK, now you got the gist of it. Let's get specific.

I guess we ought to start out with minimal traffic and then work on up to full high tide.

So for now, presume that you just got let off out in Nevada somewhere on the interstate highway at the intersection of a little dinky road that you can't see a single damn car on even though the visibility is better than a hundred miles. Needless to say, there's probably not too much more traffic on the interstate either, but oh well.

After having made the brilliant deduction that there ain't too many cars going by, your first strategy will be to get to the place with the most cars going by. A place where they can safely stop for you, I might add.

Take a look at one of these open-area ramps the next time you're out on the road. Notice how, at the downstream end of the ramp, right at the place where the last little bit of ramp disappears into the expressway, there's a paved area off the side of the expressway outside and beyond the white line that marks the edge of the driving surface. No, this isn't ALWAYS there, but 99 percent of the time will just have to do.

This is where you want to be.

Everybody on the Interstate has to go right by you and everybody (all 2 of 'em) on the little dinky side road who're entering the Interstate also have to go right by you. *Voila!* You have maximized the traffic density at the place where you are doing your hitchhiking.

That's about all there is to it when you're out in the middle of nowhere. Just be sure that there's nothing about the place you've picked that might make it a little bit more difficult for people to stop. The worst part about where you have set up shop is that everybody is cutting along at full speed and, as we all know, the faster they go the less likely they are to stop.

What makes it a situation that's not as bad as it may appear is that out in the middle of nowhere with nobody in their rear-view mirror, people are:

A) Less inclined to worry about some asshole driving up on top of their back bumper as they attempt to slow down for you, and are thus more inclined to stop.

B) More likely to be alone and in need of human conversation, therefore more willing to pick you up.

Take heart, somebody's gotta come by this godforsaken hell-hole sooner or later.

So alright already, enough about invisible towns in the middle of nothing that you'll never ever get within a hundred miles of. How 'bout something a little more relevant to a real situation that you might really find yourself in someday?

OK, we'll just stroll on over to the other end of this ramp where it connects to a honest-to-God real road traveled by respectable amounts of real people.

Notice how the ramp connects to the just plain old road.

Either it's got a regulation intersection with a regulation traffic light or stop sign where everybody's gotta come to a full, by God, stop (even in California). Or it's at the end of one of those turn lanes, where the right lane must turn right as they say, and everybody just slides on over into the turn lane and then stands on the gas pedal 'till they're up to warp speed so they can merge smoothly with the expressway traffic. As opposed to merging not-so-smoothly with the front end of that cement truck.

There's not too much that's very complicated about any of this. Mostly, the upstream end of the ramp that's farthest away from the expressway is just like a regular intersection (you've already read about that) on a regular street.

Drive around outside sometime and take a look at all this neat stuff. It's been lying there for years without you ever paying it a lick of attention. Ain't it about time you got wise to it?

If there's a traffic light or stop sign at the upstream end of the ramp, treat it just like you would any other light on any other road. Treat it like any other intersection. If there's not a safe pull-over spot downstream of the intersection, stand right next to the light or stop sign and do the routine described in the part of this book you've already read. The part about intersections. If there's not a traffic light and everybody is zooming along merging into the main flow, it's not gonna be as easy. Less easy, but not too bad, really.

Usually, there's a kind of turn or corner that cars gotta round in order to get aimed in the same general direction as the expressway before they enter it. Stay away from places like that, 'cause they're dangerous and the people driving your way know it, so they're not about to stop.

Stopping on the curve is a good way to get rear-ended by the next guy coming around the bend with his hand in his girl-friend's pants who ain't even thinking about looking where he's headed.

After all, he already KNOWS there's nothing up there in front of him that might block his way. I mean, this *is* an expressway, you know.

So stay away from the corners and bends. OK?

That's gonna put you either upstream ahead of the bend or downstream towards the dreaded expressway.

Try for upstream every chance you get. It's better. Only time to avoid upstream is, you guessed it, when there is nowhere for people to safely get their asses off the road whilst stopped to let you into their cars. Or maybe at night when there's a whole flock of streetlights people can use to see you with down at the end of the ramp on the edge of the expressway.

Give the turn lane a good looking over for some kind of smooth spot outside of the traffic lane. A spot that's a touch past where everybody has already merged into the main flow. You want it to be past where everybody's already merged so that you don't have to dodge folks that aren't too good at merging. This spot usually shows up somewhere near the end of that "must turn right" lane. Sometimes it'll be grass, but whatever it is, it wants to be nice and long with plenty of room for people to come to a stop in without banging over some kinda ledge or drop-off and then plenty more room after that for them to accelerate to a decent speed in safety before getting back into the main flow.

Plant yourself here and follow the easy-to-read instructions conveniently located elsewhere in this book that tell you how to hitchhike.

Downtown is the pits. If you find yourself stuck in a full urban location, there's not a whole lot you can do to improve things. It's doubly frustrating 'cause you can't get away from the main meat of the expressway like you can everywhere else. You don't get an on ramp with one end that's a normal road.

Both ends are full-blown expressways with cars zooming along at 80, and everybody's all pissed off and not wanting to stop for their own mothers, let alone you. Or me. The best you can do is look for a long straightaway where people can see you (and anybody who pulled over to pick you up) in time to take appropriate action.

You're probably gonna get busted by the cops before anybody stops for you, so why don't you just make your life easier by asking the guy who's got you in his car right now just exactly how much further he's going, so that you can ask him to pull over right here, thanks, before you are totally engulfed in the concrete octopus.

You'll be glad you did.

Your Appearance

OK. Now you know where to hang out so you can get rides. But what about the way you look? If we're gonna do this at all, we probably oughtta do it right. So here we go with your appearance.

Just like mom.

Stand up straight. Comb your hair. Tuck in that shirt. Where'd you get those awful shoes?

Actually, it's not gonna be like that at all.

Relax.

Maybe we'll find out why people think what they think about you. Based on the only thing they've got to go on. Your looks.

When you go driving down the road and you see somebody standing there on the roadside with their thumb out, your mind (consciously or otherwise) makes an instant decision about whether or not you'd ever let that person in your car with you. This happens even when you've got the wife and kids with you while you're on your way to church, and there's no way in hell you'd ever give anybody a ride at the time.

That instant decision is made on one thing only.

Looks.

The same thing applies to all those people sailing down the road past you as you stand there hitchhiking.

Now, it is true that some people are a little less critical than others when it comes to sizing somebody up. For the majority of people driving cars, it's enough that you look like a hitchhiker. That's it. That's all you get. You ain't getting into their car and that's all there is to it.

So we'll forget all those jerks and try to fix up our looks to suit everybody else who is:

A) a bit more critical of eye when sizing you up.

B) inclined to give somebody a ride every so often.

What you look like has a huge effect on how quickly you get picked up and who (or what) picks you up. So before you get out there on the side of the road, you want to take a little time to tailor your looks to get the most out of your situation.

There's a few different things going on at the same time and you don't want to ignore any of them.

Some of the stuff to pay attention to as regards your roadside appearance includes: Who you are, How old you are, Where you are, Who you want stopping to let you in their car, Your clothing, Your general appearance, Your stance, and a couple of other things I can't think of right now. In a nutshell, you want to tailor your appearance to suit the largest group(s) of people going by, who might reasonably be expected to stop for you, that you'd willingly get into a car with if they did stop.

I suppose we can go ahead and take this junk in the mostly random order that I just typed it in. OK?

Who are you? Good question. Lotta folks don't have a clue who they are. This piece might be a little rough for them. They have my sympathy. You, however, I'll presume *do* know.

So let's get on with it.

Are you an aging black man? Are you a sexy young Nordic blonde woman? Are you a just-plain-old-white boy? Are you intensely fat and horrifically ugly?

You can't do a damn thing about the hand God dealt you, and I wouldn't want you to even if you could. You must, however, accept the fact that your appearance critically affects your odds of getting a ride.

When hitchhiking, the saying that opposites attract goes out the window (except maybe for our Nordic blonde who's gonna attract some real winners by way of horny sailors and loony rapists). She ain't got no damn business by herself out here on the road, so we're gonna skip her. Plan on getting most of your rides with people who share a lot of similarities with you.

Young people give each other rides. So do older people, military guys in uniform (I hope you're smart enough to realize that the guy driving ain't the one that's in uniform fer chrissakes), surfers, and hairy bikers.

When you see somebody coming who looks like you or the people you hang out with, give 'em a little extra eye contact.

In my experience, the group most likely to stop consists of blue-collar-type white males driving cars that don't shine.

Whatta you think that might make me?

Yeah.

If you're not like everybody else out there you're not gonna get as many rides. It's enough to piss you off or make you bitter about life, but there it is. Reality. Just like getting beat up by a big brother your whole life and then when you finally grow up and get to be bigger than him it's not the same somehow so you leave him in one piece.

Your age is a major player in the "who's gonna pick me up?" game. So do yourself a favor and don't try to fake everybody out by wearing the latest in teen-age fashion if you're 55. If you try that NOBODY's gonna stop. The same holds true in reverse but I've never seen too many 16-year-olds out there walking around in three-piece suits, so it's probably not too much of a problem.

Where you are is another big one. Different types of people gather together in different places. I dunno why, they just do. If you're one kind of person thumbing in an area populated by some other kind of people, your odds decrease. And depending on where you're at, it might not be just your odds of getting a ride that are on the decline. Keep this in mind, wouldja?

Think ahead a little when you're deciding about where you're going and where you'd like to get dropped off to try for that next ride.

If you're a black guy decked out in the latest urban attire, you really don't want to get dropped off in the middle of Yeehaw Junction (real place) on Saturday night when Billy Bob, Betty Sue (why the hell do these people all have two first names?) and all their redneck friends are out tooling around in their 4x4's drunk on Jack Daniels.

Hopelessly white dorfs with 6 pens in the pocket of their white button-down shirts do not want to try their luck at three a.m. in South L.A.

Of course I'm overstating it here, but it's by way of trying to make a point. In truth, I've never come nowhere close to getting mugged or whatever in all my years of hitchhiking. And I've been through some pretty down-and-dirty neighborhoods.

But I don't go around looking like I'm a fat juicy target either.

Try to blend in.

One more point here about where you are, OK? About 99 percent of all the hitchhiking you'll ever do will be in places you are already familiar with to one degree or another. Looking like you belong shouldn't be any hassle at all.

You already know what you should look like.

Who you want giving you a ride is also worth considering. If you're into serious weirdos, then go ahead and let your beard grow out and wear that pink dress. If you want regular people, then try to at least look like one. You don't have to be one, you just gotta look like one. Take note, however, that there are a whole lot more regular people out there than there are serious weirdos.

Your clothes.

Now we're going to get serious. Make a little note over there in the margin that this is one of the big ones.

There's an awful lot of dumb stuff you can do by way of wearing clothes the wrong way that can keep you out of people's cars. A whole helluva lot in fact. The main deal is not so much trying to dress up or something, but to avoid clothing that repels potential rides.

I suppose it's about equal parts of lousy outfits and decent outfits that have been allowed to enter a state of lousiness through neglect or whatever that repel rides the best.

Let's do lousy outfits first. Leather pants are a lousy outfit. So is a black jacket covered in silver studs and fifty zippers. So is a white lab coat over purple shorts. So is a raincoat on a sunny day. Get-ups like this telegraph "I'm a dipshit" to everybody going by. It matters not at all that you're really not a dipshit, people are definitely going to think you're one, and you don't get a chance to talk with 'em to persuade 'em otherwise.

Full biker colors is a lousy outfit. That is, unless it's bike week down in Daytona Beach, in which case it's an EXCELLENT outfit. Bound to get a ride. Just hope it's not the Warlocks rumbling by when you're looking your Saints best. Other dumb outfits include things like huge rhinestone earrings and 10 pounds of gold chains around your neck.

The gold chains bring up another issue unrelated to your odds of getting a ride. Namely, your odds of getting beat up and robbed. Or worse. While it's just fine to dress up for your date when you're out at the steak house with her, it's definitely dumb verging on downright dangerous when you're standing alone by the side of the road on the wrong side of the tracks after dark.

Decent outfits that have become lousy through neglect or whatever are just about what you're thinking they are. Like new blue jeans and a tucked-in white pinstripe shirt with one sleeve torn off. Don't laugh! I've seen that stuff! Or one shoe. Another big winner. Clothing of any color that has been allowed to turn brown with accumulated crud is another no-no. You'd think I wouldn't have to tell you this (hell, I don't believe I've gotta tell you this), but what I see on the side of the road every day tells me I do.

Like the example of the biker colors above, lousy outfits are area-dependent. Mud-encrusted dungarees are a real turn off in Grosse Pointe, Michigan, but they're just fine in the piney woods of Mississippi (as long as you're not on Interstate 10).

I'll get a ride pretty quick standing by the side of the road in nothing more than a pair of shorts with a surfboard under my arm down here by the beach in Florida, but all I got when I tried the same thing in the desert 40 miles west of Fort Worth, Texas, was stares and laughter (but luck was with me, 15 minutes before bedding down for the night with all the rattlers and scorpions I got a ride all the way to the doorstep of the house I was going to in San Diego!).

You want to try to be wearing the kind of stuff that will fit in most anywhere in this great country of ours. Don't try to out-fancy everybody with what you're wearing. Do your standing out with your location and stance, NOT your clothes.

Hard to go wrong with good old blue jeans and a colored T-shirt with a pair of tennis shoes. At least as long as it's not one of those sweat-discolored, beer-stained, 2-sizes-too-small kinda T-shirts that dad watches TV in. Slacks are OK, long as they ain't got those knife-edge creases. If you're at the beach, look beachy (50 years old in a pair of plaid Bermuda shorts down past your knees with a Hawaiian shirt ain't beachy, by the way). If you're in the hills, look hilly. LOOK REAL.

Button-down shirts are okeydokey unless you've got a case of the machos and can't seem to button the top three buttons, so as to show off your manly chest. Nobody likes those guys anyway, with the possible exception of about 2 air-headed girls. And they're both weird, so forget 'em.

Wear something you won't mind getting dirty in (the upholstery in some people's cars is composed of 2 parts cigarette ashes mixed with 1 part motor oil). Wear something that won't look too damn rotten if it does get a little dirty. T-shirts beat tuxedos every time. Nice T-shirts. No holes.

Military uniforms are good now that we seem to have finally gotten Viet fucking Nam behind us (it's a damn shame how everybody treated those guys when they came home).

Look like somebody who never ever even thought about robbing somebody. But not a weenie.

All the nice clothes in the world ain't gonna do you a bit of good, however, if your general appearance is all fucked up. Remember all that stuff your mom kept nagging you about when you were growing up? Well, I'm gonna nag you about it too. You wouldn't think people could tell that your teeth are yellow when they're whizzing by at 65, would you? Well, they can. Even when you've got your mouth closed. Stuff like that can either keep you out of somebody's car to begin with or shorten your ride if you do manage to get in. Having scruffy long hair and a raggedy-looking beard is probably the worst offense. People just don't go for it. And you ain't gonna change the world. That's the way it is, and that's that. People associate scruffiness with unpleasantness.

If you gotta have a beard, then at least keep it neatly trimmed. Really, though, you ought to get rid of it. It keeps you from looking wholesome and all-American.

Comb the damn hair. Better yet, cut it first and then comb it.

There, that's better.

Huge tattoos showing various scenes of depravity and violence all over you are really smart too. Wear long sleeves. Even in August. Unless it's bike week.

Take a bath and use some deodorant, wouldja? You stink. If you're in the hills of Idaho on your way to Chicago, then go for a swim (with your clothes ON) in that stream over there. You'll eventually dry off and warm back up. It'll add 50 percent to the length of your rides. Minimum.

Hopefully, you packed a toothbrush. I hate people who smell up my car when they talk. Yuck. I drop all of 'em off at the next corner. "Yeah this is as far as I'm going. I forgot about having to stop here when I told you I was headed all the way to New York. I'll pick you up again if you're still here when I get back on the road. Honest."

Ignore this sage advice if you're next to a big construction site at quitting time. Those guys don't give a shit, and you probably look better than them anyway.

And now for the main event. Drum roll please.

Your Stance

Put another note in the margin here. But this time make it say this is the biggest one of all. Maybe underline it too. Yeah, that looks OK.

On the biggest expressway with the fastest traffic and you with matted hair, scraggly beard, a life-size tattoo of a skull with a snake coming out of its eye on your hairy, exposed chest, and holding a Bowie knife in your hand; yes, you, will get a ride (and pretty quick) if you take a good stance there on the roadside.

Believe it.

Actually, this part's gonna be about more than just your stance. I'll try to cover your whole physical orientation here if I can. There's a fair bit to it.

Let's start out by talking about eye contact. For some weird reason, people who need a seeing eye dog just to find their zipper when they're gonna take a leak can tell whether or not you're making eye contact with them from a mile away when they're coming at you doing 80. Day or night, rain or shine. And for some even weirder reason, if you're not making eye contact with them, they don't stop for you.

I have not the faintest idea WHY this is, but it definitely IS.

To make good eye contact, you gotta be paying attention. Hitchhiking can be awfully boring sometimes, but don't let it cause you to drift off into a stupor. Look each driver of each car that comes your way straight in the eyes. Follow his eyes as he goes by. Let him know that you're definitely watching him.

People are really funny. It's almost as if they're trying to sneak past you and if you don't look 'em squarely in the eye they think maybe you won't notice 'em or something. Part of what gets you rides is guilt. People feel guilty about motoring along in a nice comfortable car while you're out there on the side of the road breathing their fumes and choking on dust. And just like other kinds of guilty people, they won't feel as guilty if they don't get caught. So it's up to you to catch 'em.

Weird huh? But true.

However, you don't want to overdo it. If there's so much traffic that you're standing there rattling your head just to make eye contact with everybody then that's too much. Relax. Pick only as many drivers to single out for eye contact as you can handle without strain. People will notice the strain and not stop.

Deciding which ones to lock onto is worth some thought, too. I mean you can either do it totally random or try to improve your odds with people you know are a little more inclined to give you a lift. Go back and read the part about who stops for who again and pay attention this time, OK? I'll be here when you get back.

Back already? You must be a fast reader.

Those are the guys to bear down on. Don't let 'em sneak past you. Just don't try to bore a hole through 'em when you're looking at 'em, all right?

The number of people going by that you can make good eye contact with is an indicator of how much traffic is the right amount of traffic. The right amount of traffic is when you can make good eye contact with everybody going by without pulling a neck muscle. No more, no less. I know, it looks like not enough people going by, but trust me. That's just right.

Maybe a steady flow of one car every five seconds or so. That provides your very best odds for getting picked up.

Talk about eyes leads to talk about faces. Our next subject. It's kinda hard to describe how your facial expression oughtta look exactly. You want to look pleasant, hopeful, sane, fun to be around and honest all at the same time.

Looking the opposite of any of these can ruin it for you.

Guys who look like Richard Nixon should find something else to do besides hitchhike.

Again, people with 20/400 vision (that's really bad) can zero in on the look on your face from the next county at night for some reason.

If the wife you've loved dearly all your life just served you with divorce papers and you're one of those people who can't hide their feelings, then pick another day to go thumbing.

Practice your expression in the mirror if you have to (when nobody's around, of course). Look engaging. Like somebody who's probably got a million neat stories to tell.

Don't mistake any of this for good-looking.

Good-looking don't hurt any, but it's not what we're interested in here. You can project all those things I listed up there a few lines back and still be ugly as homemade dirt. If you've never really given any thought to goofy shit like this before, well, now's the time. If you can learn to do it hitchhiking, then you can also do it other places.

Just might come in real handy some day.

While we're in the neighborhood of your face, let's do your head too. So you're thinking "What the hell's wrong with my head, fer chrissakes?," right? Probably nothing, but that ain't what I'm fixing to get at. This is another one that goes under the heading (get it?) of "I can't believe that I actually gotta tell you guys this stuff." Keep your goddamned head aimed at the cars coming your way!

For some really dumb reason, a lot of the people I see on the side of the road are turned around facing AWAY(!) from traffic and trudging along in the direction of where they want to go.

This is not smart!

Everybody going by (almost) is thinking the same thing. If this guy's close enough to where he's going to be walking to get to it, then the hell with him, let him walk, I don't need to stop just to take him another 3 blocks.

Idiots like this are usually walking when they're MILES from where they're going! The ONLY time to turn around and head off downstream is when you're getting away from some really crummy spot and walking over to a really good spot. I suppose it's OK to stick your thumb out while you're doing it, but it's really useless when you think about it.

The time to start walking is when the amount of time it's probably gonna take to get a ride is less time than it's gonna take to walk to your destination. And then you're not hitchhiking anymore, are you? Putting your thumb out while walking slows you down. And when you're walking it's a lot harder for people to recognize that that's your thumb out there and that you're a hitchhiker. Either way you lose. So why do it?

Not only that, but turning around and ignoring everybody tells 'em that you don't really give a shit about them, do you? Needless to say, this plays hell with your attempts to look engaging at the very least. If I'm glomming down the road and I want somebody in my car with me to break up the boredom by talking with me, I'm sure the hell not gonna stop for some jerk who won't even look my way.

OK?

So now that we got you turned around facing the right way, let's see what we can do for you.

Believe it or not, lotsa people have a hard time figuring out just exactly what it is that you're doing out there on the side of the road. You want to fix things so that there's no doubt whatsoever in everybody's mind as to what it is you're up to out there. Not only that, but we also want people to think you're really enthusiastic about it. Real gung-ho. Everybody likes a guy who really puts his all into it. Know what I mean? Everybody wants to back a winner, so what you have to do is look like a winner.

Stand up, dammit! Absolutely no sitting, crouching, bending, stooping, hunkering down or leaning against signs permitted. If you're so damn comfortable sitting there by the roadside, then sit there. I ain't stopping for you.

No slouching, either.

Ain't this a real pain in the ass? Just like all that fucked up stuff your mother, drill sergeant, P.E. coach, whomever was all the time ragging your ass for.

But it's for a good reason. So do it.

When you look too relaxed, people don't feel as guilty going by without stopping for you as they do when you look like there's some kind of urgent reason for getting yourself a ride RIGHT NOW. Now I'm not saying that you gotta stand at attention or something. In fact, parade rest ain't necessary either. But stand up straight and stick your arm straight out with your thumb straight up. Really. Spread your feet apart a little too. And don't face exactly into the traffic. Set your right foot a little downstream like you're ready to take off running after 'em even before they bring their car to a full stop down there.

Yeah, that's it.

Maybe even lean forward into the flow a little too. Are we getting the idea here yet? Look eager! Look like some kind of innocent fellow who's on his way somewhere to get some really good news or something and really needs a ride RIGHT NOW.

Once more, OK? Stand up straight. Put your arm out straight horizontally. Close the fingers on your hand fully and keep your thumb at full attention. Straight up. Like a hard on.

No, I'm not making any of this up. I've personally tested each and every one of these little tidbits on real roads while thumbing for real rides.

42

Now, it is true that eventually you'll get a ride even if you're lying down in the grass over there with your thumb barely separated from the half-open palm of your hand while looking straight up at that cloud that looks like a big alligator with his mouth wide open, but I have to assume that if you're reading this book it's because you want to learn how to get where you're going as soon as you can.

For free.

Mind you, I've got nothing at all against hitchhiking as a pure killtime without a thought in the world about where you're even going or when you're gonna get there. That's a lot of fun, and you'll meet some real interesting people while you're doing it. Great way to spend a lazy summer's day or two.

And if that's what you've got in mind, then you can forget all this bullshit and lounge around and watch the ants dig in the dirt while the breeze blows through your hair and maybe you'll get a ride and maybe you won't and who the hell cares anyway.

Back to the story.

Where you gonna stand? Think you know? Maybe.

Maybe not.

Where you gonna stand? Sounds like a pretty stupid question, don't it? Whadda you mean "Where'm I gonna stand?," What the hell kinda dipshit question is that? I'm gonna stand over here by the road. Where all the cars are, in case you haven't noticed.

That's not bad for starters, but there's a little more to it than that. Don't stand with one foot over the white line in the traffic lane.

That's dumb for three reasons.

Reason 1 is it's illegal, and if a cop comes by he's gonna bust the shit out of you. But there are not that many cops driving by all the time, and that's not the main reason to stay the hell off the roadway.

Reason 2 is that it's dangerous to stand on the roadway. Somebody's gonna come along trying to swat that bee that just flew in the window and not see your dumb ass out there on the pavement and splatter you all the way into tomorrow's obituary section in the local paper. Mister Bee is going to enter the last seconds of your life at the exact time you turn around to get a better look at that blonde with the really tight ass over there behind you.

BLAM!

The only nice thing about the whole bloody, gutty mess will be that you never knew what hit you.

But let's face it, people don't get smeared across two lanes of traffic all that often. Which brings us to reason 3. The main one.

Reason 3 for staying off the pavement is so as you'll have a better chance of getting a ride. People don't like to get crowded. If you're crowding me, I'm not gonna think you're a very nice fellow. And I only give rides to nice fellows. Never pushy bastards who try to crowd me. People with their foot in the traffic zone are pushy bastards.

Every last one of 'em.

Can you comprehend that?

Pushy bastards don't do too good at comprehending either.

Don't go standing way over there in the weeds either. Nobody's gonna know you're even there.

So I can hear you thinking to yourself, "OK, mister smart guy, where DO I stand?"

Glad you asked.

Assuming reasonable conditions (yes, I know just how rare reasonable *anything* is), you want to be far enough away from the road that if you fell flat on your face in the direction of the pavement, you'd maybe just hit the edge of the pavement (or that white line they got that tells the drivers where out of bounds is) with your forehead. If you're doing this right, your outstretched hand won't make it to the edge of the pavement, or the line.

You're not crowding anybody (except maybe some really paranoid creep, but he wasn't gonna stop for you anyway), but you're close enough to the road that nobody's gonna miss seeing you.

This also just happens to put you far enough away from the pavement that Mister Bee will probably just miss you when he goes by with one tire off the road.

Take it from me, your heart rate won't return to normal for a week. But you'll be in one piece.

Sometimes, when you REALLY REALLY need to get somewhere in a hurry (yeah, yeah, I know, you're not supposed to ever be in a hurry when hitchhiking, but nobody's perfect), it helps to put a little body-English into your presentation. For some reason, body-English doesn't seem to work real well unless you're a little emotional about it. At least not for me. Maybe you're a better actor than I am.

Try putting your arm out towards the oncoming traffic and then taking it back along the direction that everybody's going. Start out by picking a likely ride out of the crowd (read the part about who does and who doesn't give rides) and lining up your thumb on them at eye level like a gunsight or something. As they move past you, keep your thumb right on 'em. You know, like hunters do with their shotguns when the ducks fly over.

Try to drill a hole in 'em with eye contact, too. Make your face PLEAD like you're begging for your life.

It's really funny sometimes. People will see that you've singled 'em out of the bunch and just pull right over. They get this look on their faces like you caught 'em or something, and they just pull right over.

It's kinda weird, but it works.

Have a good story ready to tell why you needed a ride so bad, and sometimes they'll go way the hell out of their way to take you where you're going. If you're going somewhere close to a hospital, then tell 'em to take you there. Your mom's sick.

Sure.

Nighttime Hitchhiking

Here's a good one. Thumbing in the dark.

Cringe.

Take heart, it's not so bad. I make no distinction between daytime or nighttime when I'm hitchhiking. If I feel like going, I go.

To hell with what time it is.

Hitchhiking at night is a matter of visibility, plain and simple. If they can't see you, they can't stop for you.

Hell, most people can't make up their minds about whether or not to stop and give you a lift in broad daylight with 20-mile visibility, so at night EVERYTHING boils down to visibility.

Got it?

Visibility comes in two flavors: bright you against dark background, and dark you against bright background. Since I can hear people muttering to themselves about how the hell can there be a bright background at night (not the smart ones like you), I'll proceed with bright you (get it?) against a dark background first.

At night there are only two light sources that people driving can use to see you: the headlights on their car, or streetlights and stuff like that. Take it from me, if you have a choice (and usually you do), fix it so streetlights and stuff like that are what makes you stand out against that gloomy background you're in front of.

Let's take streetlights. If you'll think about it a little, you'll discover that at night all streetlights make a little pool of illumination right under themselves that's brightest at the center and fades out towards the edges. Common sense will tell you that the place to stay is right smack in the middle where the light is brightest.

Forget common sense.

With the light blasting down on the top of your head as you stand directly under it, the front of you (that's the only part of you that oncoming traffic can see, remember?) remains just about as dark as that dark background behind you. The result? Dark on dark. No visibility. No ride.

So what you gotta do is to kinda strike a bargain between things getting darker as you move BACK (surely I don't gotta tell you what happens when you move forward do I?) away from the light and the light hitting you more and more squarely in the front as you move away from it. When the bargain's a good one, sometimes the result is better visibility than in daylight.

Now I'm not saying that judgment calls like this are easy to make on the first go, but a little intelligent forethought on your part coupled with some astute watching of things as you drive by at night to actually SEE what they really LOOK LIKE out there, and your odds of getting a ride at night will improve.

Street lights aren't the only roadside source of illumination, but the principles remain exactly the same. Balance your closeness to the light source against the angle in which the light hits you. Avoid a bright light source at low elevation ahead of or near you, as the glare it makes on windshields will swamp your dimly-glowing form.

As for the other source of illumination, the headlights on the car coming your way, there ain't a damn thing you can do about that except maybe hope that the drongo who's doing the driving took the time to have them properly adjusted recently, so forget 'em.

Go find a yourself a nice streetlight.

A semi-loophole around this situation exists at intersections that have a traffic light or stop sign. With people sitting there at full stop, it becomes much easier for them to see you. Also, if there's an intersection with a traffic light, it's usually because you're in town and therefore bathed in the glow of all those city lights. Take advantage of any such set-up and stay put right there. Treat it just like I described in the part about intersections. The slower they're going, the better your odds.

And while we're on the subject of visibility here, I'm gonna take this opportunity to thump the tub of "dressing the part" some more.

Stop and think a little here and tell me what kind of clothes you want to be wearing when everything you're doing is revolving around just trying to be seen? That's right, white or light colors. The brighter (not bright colors) the better. If something's gotta be dark, make sure that it's the pants.

Additionally, a good stance helps too. Stick that arm straight out there, dammit! Maybe ease in towards the pavement a little too, but

48

watch it, somebody just might pick the place where you're standing to drift off the edge of the pavement. Needless to say, if they're in no shape to stay altogether on the road, then they're probably in no shape to see you or avoid drilling you if they do see you at the last second (yours).

Always always always be ready to jump for your life.

OK, enough about that. How about dark you against bright background?

Before I go any farther here, I want to say right now that this part works just fine while you're wearing LIGHT clothes. Don't ask why, it just does. So you can quit worrying about taking 2 changes of clothing when you go hitchhiking at night. OK?

I suppose if you don't trust me you can wear a light undershirt with a dark regular shirt and just put whichever one on the outside you feel will work best.

Suit yourself.

The idea is to have a sense of what the oncoming driver sees as he looks in your direction. Keep in mind the fact that in order to see you he's gonna have to look a tickle to the right of straight ahead. We're not in England. Right? So what you want to do is to imagine yourself looking in that same direction from the point of view of all those cars coming at you.

Got it?

Good, now turn around and look at what's back there behind you in that exact same direction. Hopefully what you see is some kind of EXTENDED (you know, like all smoothed-out and definitely NOT a few blinding point sources like a half-dozen distant streetlights) glow. That extended glow can be caused by a variety of things like for instance that giant portable signboard right there behind you, the glow of streetlights shining against the white surface of a building or billboard, or even just the combined blur of a zillion different town lights way back in the distance.

Whatever it is, just be sure to position yourself EXACTLY between it and the cars coming at you, keeping in mind the fact that as the cars get closer and closer (and thus better and better able to see your pitiful ass) they're gonna be looking farther and farther off to the right, away from the direction that they're zooming along in.

Also keep in mind that whoever it is that eventually stops to give you that lift probably hasn't cleaned his windshield in a while, and all those bug guts and general smear are gonna make a healthy glare around any bright point sources of light back there almost right behind you, rendering you totally invisible, so whatever you do, don't have something bright nearly, but not quite, right behind you.

You've got two good legs (I presume anyhow), so use 'em both to POSITION yourself in a spot that MAXIMIZES your visibility. Otherwise, nobody's gonna ever see you, and then you'll have to read the chapter about picking a good (Ha Ha) spot to spend the night.

Did you bring your sleeping bag, by any chance?

Making And Using Hitchhiking Signs

Lotsa times when you're out on the road, the pavements all start looking like a bunch of spaghetti strands going all over the place every which way. No sane grid pattern, just a bunch of curvey-wurvey stuff that heads off one way and then changes its mind later on and decides to go somewhere else.

Real pain in the ass.

Hard as hell for people to figure out where you're going.

Times like this are times when you need a sign.
A good one.

When people aren't too sure about where you're going, it's a lot easier for them to blow right on by without feeling guilty about not stopping for you, 'cause they can rationalize in their pointy little heads that you're not going where they're going so it's OK to leave you back there on the side of the road eating their dust.

And if that's not enough, then what's even better is when somebody actually DOES stop for you and then you go about a quarter mile and they start heading north when you want to go south so they drop you off in some really awful spot where NOBODY can get on or off the road in one piece.

So now you're REALLY stuck and you'll probably never get to that hot-looking-girl-you-met-yesterday's place where you just know she's sitting there on the couch watching TV in a long T-shirt down to the tops of her delicious thighs and nothing else and wondering where the hell are you anyway and maybe she'll call her old boyfriend instead and... well you know, really terrible stuff that'll make you break out in prickly heat all over just thinking about it.

So you gotta have a sign.

Signs tell prospective rides where you're off to and make 'em feel real guilty about not stopping for you when they're going to the same damn place.

I used 'em all the time in San Diego, where the roads are a jumbled mess and everything's 30 miles from everything else.

Worked real good too.

So OK, let's do signs, then.

A sign has only one job in its life, and all that is, is to COMMUNICATE to people going by in cars where it is that you're going.

As simple as that little dab of work is, you'd think that doing a sign would be pretty easy, huh?

No such luck, Bobo.

People have a God-given talent for horsing up the easiest of easy tasks, and signs fall squarely in the middle of that unfortunate category.

Despite all the stuff I've told you about elderly legally blind people being able to note the expression on your face in the dark at 80 miles an hour from the next town (all true true true), most people don't do too well with signs unless they're (the signs, that is) really clear and easy to read.

And come to think of it, considering the pitiful state of literacy in this country, maybe nothing is easy to read. So let's concentrate on that then, OK?

We'll do clarity first. Clarity as in making the letters so that people can recognize them.

52

Do you know how to do those big block letters? You know, the kind that have fat straight lines. If not, then you better start practicing now so you'll be good enough to draw (that's right, DRAW) them boogers when you need to.

This ain't art class and you don't get extra credit for making fancy letters.

There's only one kind of lettering that's allowed on hitchhiking signs and that's BLOCK.

Period.

Do NOT use line letters. Never. Ever.

Even though *you* can see that heavy line that a magic marker makes, nobody else can. Especially people zipping past you in cars with dirty cracked windshields.

Draw the outline of each letter in a nice well-proportioned block style and then fill them suckers in all the way and keep the edges nice and neat.

And make sure that you use something like black letters on a white background. The highest brightness contrast you can get. Not color contrast. Stay away from colors every chance you get. Colors are probably the worst thing you can use. Maybe a really really dark red or something on a BRILLIANTLY white background, but not if you can help it. Black letters against white is without a doubt the best.

Really.

Spend extra time on your lettering. Neatness definitely counts here. Besides, if you're like most people, you'll have occasion to use that sign more than once. So do a good slow solid job on the letters, do it right, and then save the sign for next time.

But don't moosh it all up in a little wad before you stick it in your designated stash place. If you go doing that, then all that people driving by will see is a crumpled up mess with some kind of hieroglyphics on it, no matter how neat the letters were when you first made it.

Fold it neatly with the fold lines running between (not through) letters or words.

And no script. Never. Always always always use printing.

Take a look around at all the signs and stuff around you and pick out the dullest, plainest, clunkiest kind of letters and try to make your sign just like that.

Needless to say, the bigger the letters, the easier they are to read from a distance. And the farther away folks can read 'em, the better your chances are that they'll decide to stop for you.

So what are you gonna use for a signboard anyway? I suppose it would be nice if we could get one of those big sandwich signs that people walk around in with 3' x 5' boards on their front and back sides with straps going over their shoulders to hold the whole thing together.

That'd be really neat 'cause it's big enough to put the full street address of where you're going on it along with the phone number, zip code and directions for how to get there. Plus it'd be a really good attention-getter, too.

But I don't think that's really what you've got in mind, do you?

So alright already, what's lying around the apartment anyway? We'll use some of that instead.

54

Most anything will do, really. All it's gotta be is light enough to hold up without wearing out your arm, reasonably flat, stiff enough so that it won't flap around in the breeze and lightly-shaded enough to be nice and contrasty to make those block letters you're gonna write with a BLACK magic marker really stand out.

And if you're smart enough to come up with a single short word (or two) that exactly expresses where it is you're going, then it doesn't really gotta be too dangblasted big either.

A piece of white construction paper will do nicely. So will a plain sheet of notebook paper that's taped to a piece of cardboard box or something like that (trimmed with scissors or a knife to the same size, please) to keep it from blowing all over the place.

Just plain old cardboard will do in a pinch, but since it's not white you gotta pay extra special attention to making the letters really clear and neat and big and really BLACK.

What I used to get from my friend's house in Ocean Beach to El Cajon and back was a plain white paper plate.

No shit, I really did.

Had "El Cajon" on it with the El right above the Cajon. It folded in half real nice with the fold line between the words and it fit in the waistband of my shorts when I wasn't using it.

It also did something else all good signs should do, too. It fit real good in the palm of my hand with just the ends of my two little fingers holding it. Everybody could easily see my whole hand stuck right out there with my thumb up in the universal sign of "I need a ride" and also see the sign telling 'em where I was going loud and clear right there next to my upturned thumb without having to look around somewheres for it too.

Worked like a champ.

Of course, you don't HAVE to have a sign that fits on your thumb hand. Another nice way to carry a sign is to hold it by the bottom edge with your left hand right in front of you at somewhere around waist level.

I've even seen guys that taped a piece of string to their signs and hung 'em around their necks. Really. Looked a little dippy but it freed up their left hands for serious nose picking and stuff.

Now let's make the lettering to where somebody can read it. Let's make the letters as big as we can.

The best way to make your letters as big as you can get 'em is to put as few of 'em as ABSOLUTELY NECESSARY on your sign. This also makes the sign easier to read, 'cause the words are shorter.

So use up every bit of space on your sign that you can, and keep the words short while you're doing it. You don't want to cram the letters of each word together or run out of room at the end of a word and have to put the last three letters in the same amount of space you used for the first one. Cheat a little and count the letters in each word before you start putting 'em down. That way you'll know that the third letter in a five-letter word goes right smack in the middle.

Don't bunch the words together, either. Whether you believe it or not, the spaces between (and above and below) the words count for a lot too.

So let's get back to as few letters as are absolutely necessary, OK? The two ways to do that are by reducing the amount of words to an absolute minimum and by reducing the amount of letters in each word to an absolute minimum.

Let's do the amount of words first.

The fewer words the better. Period. As long as it still makes sense. If there's a way to say the same thing two different ways, pick the one with the fewest words.

That paper plate with El Cajon on it serves as a good example. Everybody in San Diego knows what El Cajon is and where El Cajon is too. That was EVERYTHING they needed to decide whether or not they wanted to pick me up or not. Anything extra just confuses things.

If you're going to some little hole-in-the-wall place that hardly anybody knows about, then don't lock up on trying to come up with a way to explain it to everybody. Skip that and use the name of some place on the same road (preferably, but not absolutely necessarily, past your stopping point) that everybody DOES know about. One with a short name.

We'll stay with that paper plate a little while longer so that we can use it for an example of how this works.

I used to work at the Bullock's department store out in Fashion Valley (real place) when I lived in San Diego, and when I wanted to thumb home from work I used my El Cajon sign to get me there.

I didn't live in El Cajon, but Normal Heights (honest, that was really the name of the place) wouldn't fit on the plate and NOBODY knew where the hell Normal Heights was anyway. A bonus came from the fact that El Cajon was a pretty good throw beyond Normal Heights (I've wondered how they came up with that name all my life but I've never found out. Maybe somebody who reads this book knows and they'll write me a letter telling me all about it), and when people stopped for me, they were either going to El Cajon or close to it. Either way it was a straight-shot single-ride deal all the way home.

Almost never got stuck half-way.

In the other direction, from home to work, I used the flip side of the plate. Yeah, you get to put stuff on BOTH sides of the sign. How 'bout that? The stuff on the side of the sign that ain't showing, ain't showing. So it's OK to have stuff on both sides.

Anyhow, the flip side of my paper plate (damn, I never thought I'd get so much mileage outta that stupid sign) allows me to talk a little more about keeping things clear by choosing clearly understandable words that are short. And the words on the flip side weren't even words they were so short.

They were "O.B."

That's all.

I wrote it with the O.B. at right angles to the El Cajon on the other side. That way, the fold line between the El and the Cajon without touching the words also went between the O. and the B. without touching the letters, except it went up and down between the O. and the B. 'cause you can't get a fold to go side to side between O.B.

Everybody in good old San Diego just knew that O.B. stands for Ocean Beach. Everybody. Or at least all the ones who might stop to give me a ride.

Of course, O.B. was a good long throw past the Bullock's store where I worked, so all the stuff that applied when I was heading home also applied when I was going to work.

Pretty nifty, huh? Not only that, but Ocean Beach was where I went when I wanted to go surfing. Go to O.B., take a left (onto a road that went only one place, so no more need for a sign) and 10 minutes later I'm out in the line-up at Lobster Lounge or some other happening surf spot.

That's a hell of a lot of different uses for one lousy paper plate.

I'm not saying that your sign will treat you as well, but it'll help. And if you're careful about it, and put a little thought into it before you make it, you'll go miles and miles with it.

In half the time.

After You're Inside The Car

So OK. Now you're an expert. You know it all, so there's no point in reading any more of this crap. Just a bunch of words from here on out. Blah blah blah. Who the hell needs it anyway?

Right?

Wrong!

There's the small matter of what are you gonna do now, now that you're in the car? I bet you didn't even think about that part, did you? Figures. Nobody does. I presume you're thinking to yourself something like, "What the hell's he talking about now, I got the ride didn't I?" Well, as it turns out, there's a whole bunch of stuff you can do after you got the ride. Helpful stuff.

It basically boils down to two things:

1) Extending the ride beyond the place the person who picked you up was originally going to.

2) Keeping from getting tossed out of the car before the person who picked you up gets to where they said they were going to take you to.

Is it just me, or does EVERYTHING in this book boil down to "just two things"?

Before we do any of this, there's one more small item to attend to. One that will put your ride in a better frame of mind so you can wheedle 'em out of that extra ten miles.

Running to the car after it stops.

I have no idea why this works, but if you don't run (or if you're fat and out of shape, at least waddle as quick as you can) to the car, the guy driving gets an attitude.

People are weird.

I guess they don't like sitting there on the side of the road waiting for you to get your worthless ass into their car any longer than they absolutely have to.

Kinda makes sense if you think about it. Sorta. Your ride's gone to the trouble to stop the car and pull off the road, the least you can do is go to the trouble to keep him from waiting any longer than he must. If he decides you're a lazy asshole, you can forget all about enhancing your chances.

So run, don't walk, to the car, OK? Besides, you need the exercise.

Back to the story.

We'll start out this discussion of what goes on after you're in the car by doing the part about extending the ride, but first we need to understand a little bit about why people stop for us in the first place. It's not as simple as it looks on the surface. There are almost as many reasons as there are people. But not quite, thank God.

People generally give strangers rides 'cause they either feel guilty about not stopping or 'cause they want a little companionship. Both of these can be exploited to extend a ride.

Most times when somebody stops to pick me up, it's because they want to talk.

Take note of the fact that I did not say they wanted to hear me talk.

Most of the time, people's ideas of what constitutes a conversation add up to them talking and you listening. And so, in a weird sort of way, it turns out that a significant part of being a good hitchhiker is actually being a good conversationalist.

Goofy, huh?

Goofy or not, if you can draw your ride into a good conversation, you stand a decent chance of extending your ride.

So what's a "good conversation?"

Elementary, my dear Watson, it's whatever they want to say or hear.

The trick is quickly figuring out what it is that somebody is interested in, and then giving the impression of a deep interest in that very thing. NO MATTER WHAT. And holy shit, you would NOT believe some of the fucked-up things that people go on and on and ON about. The absolute dorfyest, retardedest, self-contradictoriest, utterest horseshit I've ever heard in my life has come from people who picked me up hitchhiking.

Without the slightest doubt.

If you're trying to make the proposition that nothing in life is free, then it's somewhere around in here that you might persuade me to agree that hitchhiking isn't completely free.

Sometimes you get a headache from listening to the bilge that spews from the mouths of hopelessly ignorant people. That and trying to keep things flowing along smoothly.

Some of my ironworker friends would call this "kissing ass" or "sucking ass" and who knows, maybe they're right. It certainly bears a strong resemblance to sucking up to the boss at work.

If you're one of those macho types who has a problem with the perception of ass kissing, you're probably gonna flunk conversation 101. And not get too damn many rides an inch past where your ride was headed in the first place. Never mind getting dumped out early on a regular basis.

I suppose, like everything else, it all depends on your point of view. As long as I'm doing it 'cause I want to do it, then it's OK with me. After all, nobody's making me stand out there on the shoulder of the road. It's my choice and I sure the hell don't have to if I don't want to. Not quite the same as at work, where serious ass kissing can mean the difference between a raise and an unemployment check. That's a pressure situation, whereas hitchhiking most definitely ain't. I can sure the hell leave it as quick as I can take it.

And besides, what's the big deal anyway? Is it really THAT important that you be right and they be wrong? And rub their noses in it to boot? So what if they're fucked up? It don't cost a nickel extra to listen instead of shout.

And who knows, you just might, God forbid, learn something. Even if it's nothing more than a finer appreciation of how the mind of some looney really works. And remember, anything you learn by mistake in the process of beating somebody out of an extra 10 miles is the purest of pure gravy. I mean, it's not even why we're out here, is it?

So relax, would you?

OK. Now that we've decided that we're not sacrificing our manhoods by being a good conversationalist, how we gonna do it?

Easy. Just don't argue. And while you're not arguing, ask just enough questions to draw out your ride without making him/her think you're dominating the discussion.

A "how's that work?" here, and an "Is that right, what'd they do that for?" there, will work wonders. If you've never bothered to learn how to do this (it's called "having an intelligent conversation") before, it's gonna take some practice to get good at it. We won't talk about what kind of self-centered asshole you must be.

So get out there and start.

All they can do if you fuck up is to not take you any farther than they were going anyway or, at the very worst, drop you off right now. And then you'll know what not to say next time.

No big deal.

Keep things light and easy. Save the heavy shit for the boys at the local union hall. Allow yourself to be made fun of.

Learn to laugh at yourself. Convincingly.

Be inquisitive.

Don't be judgmental. Go against your own beliefs, if that's what it takes to keep Señor Blabbermouth happy and talking.

Give the impression that you're really learning something for the first time that you've wanted to know about all your life.

If your ride thinks he's saving your life by imparting his one and only true version of the truth to you, he's likely to drive right past his house and take you all the way to yours, just to make sure that you really understand it. Why bust his bubble?

Sometimes this can take extreme forms.

Once I found myself hopping out of a car at Sebastian Inlet with a surfboard, miles past where the guy said he was going when he picked me up, solemnly affirming that yes, I probably SHOULD quit surfing and get a job, and thanking my ride for showing me the light.

With a straight face.

I guess that, short of being black and agreeing to join the Klan, whatever works is fair. Come to think of it, if you can pull THAT ONE off, then more power to you.

I can't count how many times I've sworn to accept the love of our savior Jesus or some such similar nonsense. It does however, sure the hell work. And I've learned a whole lot about the Bible. Comes in handy with those hard-shell Baptists (but not when I'm hitchhiking). Fucks 'em up when you know your way around their instruction manual and can give as good as you get.

We getting the picture here yet?

Another way to extend a ride is to know a whole bunch (or at least pass yourself off as knowing a whole bunch) about something that your ride is interested in. However, you have to be careful about this, as it involves you doing most of the talking. Most folks don't go for that even when they say they do.

A lot of people who think they're good storytellers ain't. It all comes down to being able to ACCURATELY judge the response of your listener. More people than I'd like to believe fall into this category. They take the slightest politeness as unbridled approval and ignore everything else. They think they're bringing the house down when all that's happening is that everybody is hoping the roof falls in on 'em.

We should ALL get better at saying SHUT UP! and not feeling bad about it.

Anyhow, if you ARE one of the few who can regale an audience, then you've got a leg up on hitchhiking. When there's a really funny story being told that somebody KNOWS has a really good ending, chances are quite good that he'll just keep on driving 'till you finish it. Right there in front of your place. This, more than anything else (with the possible exception of working live on stage), will teach you timing.

Another fucking bonus! Free.

All of this goes hand in hand with keeping from getting tossed out of the car early. Getting dropped off prematurely happens more often than you might think. If you're one of those gizorks with double extra-coarse sensibilities, then it's happened a bunch of times already and you were just too stupid to know what it was that was going on.

Suddenly the guy behind the wheel says, "Oh shit I forgot, I gotta stop here and take care of some business." Yeah, sure thing.

But it's your own damn fault anyway, so don't blame the guy for lying to you, OK? Somewhere along the line you failed to ACCURATELY gauge his responses to what you were saying, and got the old heave ho as a result. You said or did something that made him decide that he didn't really want you in his car anymore.

It IS his car.

Stop and think for a minute (yes, I know that's tough to do, but try it anyway) about the kinds of things that cause you to think that somebody's an asshole. These are basically the things you do not want to be doing if you're riding along in somebody's car as a hitchhiker.

Don't laugh at a serious proposition that your ride makes (no matter how far off the wall it really is). Don't antagonize him. Don't talk endlessly about stuff he couldn't care less about, or worse, stuff he disagrees with. Don't tell him he's ugly or smelly, even if he is. Don't go on about what's wrong with the kind of car he's driving and how he oughtta get a (fill in the blank) instead. Don't say that Republicans are all a bunch of money-grubbing thieves after he just extolled the virtues of Richard Nixon. Don't say that religion's just a crock of shit when he asks you if you know Jesus.

Is this difficult to understand?

To me, all this is pretty fucking self-evident, but from what I've seen of other folks, I'm in a small minority.

Be nice, wouldja!

And don't stink or cut smelly farts either. That's one of the few things that they can't tell about you before they stop to pick you up. Bad breath is definitely out. Nobody likes it. Not even other people with bad breath. Remember all that garbage I harangued you about back in the part about your appearances? Well, that doesn't just go away when you get inside the car. It still applies.

When properly seen to, your behavior can have a major impact on how far a ride will take you. So pay attention and don't fuck up.

Part Three: Danger And Annoyances: Shit To Watch Out For

This is the part of the book where you find out about stuff that can either bother you or hurt you. It's a mean old world out there and it's just loaded with stuff that can get you. Hopefully, after reading this, that won't happen too much.

We'll start out with the world itself. You know, weather and critters and stuff like that. Then we'll go on to traffic, and then finish up with people. OK?

Weather Hazards

I'll start with the weather. A very unboring subject when it feels like coming after you with death in its eye.

First, let's talk about what the weather can do to your own personal self. You know, like in how you can freeze to death and fun stuff like that. If you let it, the weather will really do a serious number on you.

Serious.

Anybody who ventures out on the road hitchhiking had better have some smarts when it comes to the weather. Your pitiful ass is sure the hell right out in the middle of it where it can really get to you, so you'd better have a touch of that good old all-American Abe Weatherwise savvy. Smarts about things like what the looks of the sky right now means is gonna happen later. Smarts about paying attention to the radio when the guy starts droning on about this afternoon's forecast and the outlook for tomorrow. Smarts about the odds of getting rained on while out on the road and what to do if that happens.

Common sense again.

Damn. That common-sense shit keeps coming back, over and over. Can't get away from it. Better learn how to get good at it then, huh? Yeah.

Before I go any further here, I'm gonna make it clear that this is NOT a book about the weather. I will assume that you have the minimal intelligence required to go find out about the weather on your own if you're not already in tune with things meteorological. And don't try to fool yourself about it. If you don't know, go find out. It may keep you out of the obituary column in the local paper some day.

How much you want to be attuned to the weather is directly related to where you are, where you're going (and how long that's likely to take), and what time of year it is.

If you're in Honolulu, heading to Wahiawa (why anybody'd want to go to Wahiawa is beyond me but it's not my problem) out in Hawaii, then you don't really need to pay a whole hell of a lot of attention to what's going on in the sky around you. In case you didn't know, out in Hawaii they don't really have any weather. Except for rain. They get plenty of rain sometimes, and maybe a hurricane once every 25 years or so, but that's about it.

If you're in Indiana, however, it's a whole different ball game. You'd better keep an eye on things. You can wake up on a fine sunny morning in April to shirtsleeve weather and hit the road, only to realize an hour later that the temperature has dropped below freezing and you aren't dressed for it. And that's AFTER the lightning tried to fry you and the tornado passed by a scant half-mile away and the hail pounded you and the rain drenched you. Although it ain't likely, it can become a life-and-death situation. And when it's YOUR life it gets pretty hairy.

I picked a guy up early one morning between Orlando and Disneysludge (there used to be a between, now it all kind of gloms together into one undifferentiated mass of plastic and aluminum) who was dressed in a light short-sleeved shirt with jeans and tennis shoes.

That's all.

He had just the day before arrived in Florida from up north somewhere and had dressed in what he thought was appropriate style. The goddamn temperature the previous night, he'd slept through under an overpass had dropped to seventeen fucking degrees! He didn't die from hypothermia that night, but some other folks around the state DID. I took him all the way to Tampa and I'll never know if that's really where he was going or whether he just wanted to stay warm in the car as long as possible. He was one sorry-looking specimen when he piled into the seat beside me. He couldn't get over what he'd just lived (barely) through.

People DO freeze to death outdoors. And in some very unlikely times and places, too. They also get killed by lightning. And tornadoes. And floods. Hitchhiking is NOT an indoor sport.

Is this soaking in?

If you plan on hitchhiking around your local area, then you really shouldn't need me to tell you about what the weather might or might not do. You should already know. If you don't, then you've been spending way too much time indoors, and you oughtta start getting outside more often. Out where the weather is.

Let's do rain. Rain is probably the most likely bad weather phenomenon that can befall you. It's also among the safest. I've never heard of anybody being killed by rain, but who knows? Never mind.

The one thing that rain WILL do to you is keep you from getting a ride. If you're standing on the roadside soaking wet in a rainstorm, nobody's gonna stop for you.

Pisser, huh?

But it's true. Rain can also sneak up on you with zero warning if you let it. If it looks like it might rain, be sure to have your ride let you out of the car someplace where there's something nearby you can take shelter in or under.

Overpasses are good. So are gas stations and places like that. 'Specially if you got change to buy a Coke with so the manager won't throw you off the property.

People don't want some squishy guy getting in their car and ruining the upholstery, so it's your job to be sure that particular bad dream can never happen when it's you that's hitchhiking.

One exception is when it's JUST started raining and there are drops of water on everything but nothing's wet yet. Needless to say, this doesn't last long, but it's probably the very best time of all to be hitchhiking.

People driving by can't seem to resist stopping to pull some poor shlub (that's you) off the roadside to keep him from getting soaked. Their guilt quotient goes way up for a little while. Take advantage of it every time it happens.

And it doesn't really matter where you are, either. All that noise about picking the right spot to hitchhike from goes out the window for the 5 or 10 minutes that it takes a rainstorm to set in. When you feel those first drops hitting you, stop where you are and give it your best pleading face.

Never misses.

Just mind the blind curves and stuff, OK?

Don't want the guy who picks you up to be driving an ambulance.

Along with the rain, sometimes comes lightning. Lotsa times it comes ahead of the rain. Sometimes it comes without rain.

DON'T FUCK AROUND WITH THE LIGHTNING!

It'll get your ass for sure.

Standing out there by the road all by yourself, you just happen to be the tallest object around in your spot.

Lightning LOVES the tallest object in its own little spot.

Get the hell out of there. NOW!

Lightning is one of those weird hazards that people don't pay serious attention to for some reason. Oh yeah, I know they get scared of it lotsa times, but they never seem to actually DO anything about it when it comes along. They just keep on playing golf or laying on the beach or HITCHHIKING as though it didn't really matter.

CRACK! BOOOM!

And then I guess it doesn't matter. Dead people don't give a shit what happens.

Go to the library some day and ask the reference librarian where the stuff about mortality rates for various causes is. You go reading that shit and it'll give you a whole new outlook on life. While you're in there, notice just how infinitesimally-few people actually manage to get themselves killed hitchhiking. Compare hitchhiking with serious hazards like taking a bath (I am definitely NOT kidding here) and similar situations.

Lightning gets a LOT of people.

DON'T FUCK WITH THE LIGHTNING!

Another weather bad guy is the cold. If it's really cold out, you better be covered for it. How many hours can YOU stand outside in a howling wind at minus 10 and not get hypothermia and die? Now I know that if it's 10 below you're probably not gonna get out there in it to hitch a ride, but I also know that it might have been a relatively balmy 30 above when you started out. If the Arctic front comes through when you're out there exposed to it, you're gonna pay. And it just might be the max.

This applies double to folks from the South who don't really know what the hell's going on when it comes to cold weather.

West Yellowstone can drop to freezing overnight in June if it really wants to. You go thumbing across country (which I highly recommend as a way to see America, by the way) in warm weather, and don't bring warm clothes along, you just might get a big fat surprise.

One benefit of cold weather is that it raises the guilt quotient of people. If they think you might be in trouble out there (and chances are that you are, whether you know it or not), they're gonna stop for you. Good for extending rides, too.

Another cheerful item to add to this list is heat.

Heat stroke is real.

Ever see anybody with it?

I have.

It's scary.

If it's not dealt with quickly, the guy dies. Cold liquids and lots of 'em are the best remedy for heat stroke. Lie down in the shade and don't move. Hope there's some available if it's your turn.

Don't bundle up in a whole bunch of fancy clothes to try to make people think you're respectable when it's hot. Better you should remain rideless in your shorts than die in your tux.

This is another one for long-distance thumbers to watch out for. You think it's hot in Florida and you know all about it, and then head cross-country to California, you got a real education waiting for you in Arizona. I don't give a shit how bad 99% humidity feels like at 95 degrees in Florida, it doesn't even come close to 122 degrees (yes, it really gets that hot sometimes) out in the desert. Even if the humidity IS only 6%. Plan ahead. Scout the territory before you go there. Try to find out a little about places BEFORE you're stuck there for a day. Or three.

Flooding is probably not much of an issue (how many of you guys are planning on walking into a surge of water that may be deeper than you are tall?) with one peculiar exception that not many people experience or bother to think of. That exception comes when you must overnight in the countryside and sleep where you got left by the last ride. Don't laugh, flash flooding can occur with zero rain at your particular location. A 6-foot wall of water churning your way with trees, cars, houses and who the hell knows what else in it is something you don't really want to mess with if you can avoid it.

Stay out of obvious low places and dry stream/river channels. This sort of thing is more of a problem in the dry areas out West, but it's not restricted to those places only. The sneaky part comes in when you look around and everything's dry as a bone with bushes and stuff growing all over the place.

A severe thunderstorm that dumps 5 inches of rain on a small drainage basin in 2 hours, 10 miles uphill of your present location, doesn't care if the ground you're lying on hasn't been underwater in 5 years. That wall of water's coming, and if you don't take the minimal precautions required to avoid it, you too will be listed among the dead in tomorrow's paper. If they find your body.

Hail is another good one. One in a zillion chance, but if it's YOUR lucky day it might get you a trip to the hospital.

Out in Kansas where there's zero cover for light years and wonderful conditions for severe thunderstorm development in the spring and summer when you're passing through (nobody actually GOES there), softball-sized hailstones coming down on you is a life-threatening situation. Don't believe me? Get your buddy to drop chunks of ice as big as your fist on you from the top of the highest building in town.

See what I mean?

We won't even TALK about tornadoes. Forget it. If you were meant to get sucked into the sky at 300 miles an hour and then get thrown back to the ground in the next county, there's nothing in this book that's gonna do you a damn bit of good.

Just don't stand so close to me, would you?

OK, enough cheerful stuff. Let's change the subject to what the weather can do to your local environment, such as the road and the cars on it.

We'll start with fog. Betcha didn't even think of that, didja?

Fog is a pain in two ways. It'll keep you from getting a ride. And it might even get you killed.

When the fog sets in, the folks coming your way have even less of a chance of seeing you than they did otherwise. Except for that guy five miles away who can see the shitty expression on your face and won't stop for you as a result, of course. So you gotta do everything in your power to make yourself visible.

Not an easy task.

If it's foggy at night, forget it. Go to the chapter on sleeping out in the outdoors.

Daytime fog is a stink deal too, but at least it's not hopeless. Pretty damn close, but not utterly hopeless. Just like at night (no, not in the fog), you've gotta figure out a way to stand out against the background. About the only thing you can really do is to appear as DARK as you can.

Yes, dark! On a foggy day, everything takes on a kinda washed-out, bright hazy look. Things fade into a pale gray background. Pale is the key word here. Dressing darkly is the only thing you can do to give yourself the contrast you'll need to stand out against that light gray background. Yes, I know that you're not in the habit of hitchhiking with 3 changes of clothes, but oh, well. You'll think of something.

Do NOT stand closer to the road so they'll see you better. You come through their windshield after they've slammed you and they'll see you just fine. This, you don't want.

It also leads us to the part about how fog can get you killed.

People driving cars don't have the most sterling of records when it comes to staying on the pavement in brilliant daylight. Needless to say, in the fog they're gonna be a bit less good at it.

STAY AWAY FROM THE PAVEMENT.

Besides, if you crowd the pavement, the ride you get won't take you to where you're going. I've never yet had an ambulance driver stop when I said, "Let me out here."

Another fun weather thing that can alter your immediate surroundings drastically is ice. Ice is really nice to skate on and about the best thing in the world for putting in your drink on hot afternoons. Ice storms make everything look really neat and all sparkly and crystallized, and as long as you don't have to go anywhere and can just stay indoors sipping hot chocolate (or whatever) and look at everything, they're really cool.

Otherwise, ice sucks big time.

It's useless.

I hate it.

When hitchhiking, ice forces you to look at where you're standing in a whole different way. Patches of ice on the road anyplace where cars passing near you can encounter it are serious shit. Remember all that stuff I told you about where to stand so your odds of getting a ride would be better? Well, if there's any ice in the vicinity, you can forget it.

The ice wins.

Every goddamned time.

Go somewhere else.

Ice on the road upstream of you where cars will be hitting their brakes to slow down to stop for you is about as welcome a sight as a case of the clap. Dodging some car headed towards me sideways at forty miles an hour ain't my idea of a good time. You, of course, can decide for yourself. My advice is to look real close for ice on the road upstream for a good long ways. And the shit's hard as hell to see sometimes. It's sneaky. Gotta look real close.

Ditto for the same distance downstream. A car that's upside down in the ditch behind you doesn't qualify for very much when it comes to taking your freezing ass off the side of the road and down to all that nice juicy warmth at your girlfriend's.

Water on the road's not nearly so much of a problem. If the water's deep enough to cause problems, it's also deep enough to be soaking you as carloads of grinning fools go by and splash the shit out of you. You're not gonna even be there.

Are we done with the weather? Yes. Saint Elmo's Fire is not a part of this discussion.

Animals

So let's skip to animals.

Animals are definitely something to be aware of when hitchhiking. They've pretty much got you where they want you. Out in the open with nobody around to help you out.

I'm gonna deliberately ignore dogs. If you haven't learned how to deal with dogs somewhere along the line during your life, then you probably don't want to be hitchhiking in the first place. You've been staying indoors way too much. Have a stick or something handy for dogs. Besides, most dogs are pretty stupid, and will probably just lope out into the traffic and get splattered before causing you any serious trouble.

You already know all about this.

Dogs, however, aren't the only game in town when it comes to animals that can annoy or hurt you.

Do you know what all the poisonous snakes of North America look like? No? What the hell's wrong with you, then? EVERYBODY should know what rattlers, copperheads, moccasins (also known as cottonmouths), and coral snakes look like. Everybody.

How the hell hard is it to remember what four lousy snakes look like? If you don't know, then just stay away from ALL snakes. Don't kill 'em. Just stay away from them.

Easy enough for you?

Really, it boils down to knowing what rattlers look like. Those other guys generally hang out in places that you're not gonna be dealing with while hitchhiking. Even if you gotta sleep in the great outdoors overnight.

One very good reason to know your snakes is so that if you get bitten by one, you'll know whether or not to have a hissy fit. Makes the paramedic's job easier too. Snake antivenom comes in a variety of flavors, and you don't really want to have to get all of 'em if you don't really need to. Be able to identify the sonofabitch that slides soundlessly through the grass behind you and decides to have a go at your leg.

While we're at it, don't have the hissy fit either. The more you run around and get your blood really pumping, the more the venom gets distributed throughout your body. Take it easy and stand in the middle of the road and flag down the next car. When you tell 'em what happened, they'll take you right to the nearest hospital.

Out in the country, rattlesnakes can get real populous. They generally like to hang out in holes and under rocks, but sometimes they get right out in the middle of things. Keep an eye out for rattlers when you're out in the deserts of West Texas or the scrub pine country of Florida. Although almost nobody ever actually dies of snakebite, it can be a major inconvenience, to say the least.

Down in Florida they have pygmy rattlers that are about as big as a pencil. Don't be fooled. They won't kill you, but they sure the hell CAN cause the doctor to have to amputate your finger or toe to prevent the spread of gangrene after the venom kills all the tissue in the area of the bite. Don't want to do THAT! What the hell was God

thinking about when he invented pygmy rattlers? Camouflaged pencils with poison fangs. What a concept!
  Pay attention to the snakes, OK?

Insects can also be a problem. If you're like me and allergic to bees, wasps and such-like, they'll kill you. Last time I took a hit from a wasp, it was a trip in the ambulance down to the hospital with an oxygen tube up my nose and a guy asking me "Can you breathe OK?" about every two minutes.
  Annoying as all hell, but better than suffocating from swelling inside my lungs, which is what they said would have happened if they hadn't given me the shots of antivenom and stuff. I've got a little kit I can inject myself with if I get popped again that I carry around with me all the time. The cops just LOVE that fucker. Think it's some kind of works for hitting myself up with heroin or something. Real conversation piece.
  If you're allergic, take the kit with you when you go hitchhiking. Never mind the cops. Eventually somebody with an IQ above 40 will show up at the station house and sort it all out.

This is another opportunity for me to thump the hitchhiking safety tub. Compare the figures on how many people get killed from hitchhiking each year with how many die of bee stings.
  The bees win.

Fire ants are no small item either. I'm allergic to them too. Just a lucky kind of guy. Even if you're not allergic to 'em, they can cause serious trouble. You go laying your blanket on a fire-ant mound on a cold dark night when they're all immobilized from the cold, you're gonna get a real wake-up call when your body heat or tomorrow's sun warms 'em up.

Look close for 'em, the bastards are smart. When you step into their mound without noticing what you're doing, they all crawl up in your pants without letting you know they're there, and when there's a zillion of 'em there they all start biting at the same time on some mysterious secret signal.

If you're from up north and you think you know all about red ants, stop right here. Fire ants are NOT red ants. They're much, much more bothersome than red ants. Be careful.

Spiders, scorpions, centipedes and such all are pretty much self-explanatory. Black widows are something you should already know about so I won't go on and on about them; brown recluse's (also known as fiddlebacks for the distinctive violin-shaped mark on their very nondescript bodies) are something else altogether. Even though they're probably more poisonous than black widows, hardly anybody seems to know about 'em. Just a little ole brown spider. The good part is you'll never see 'em outdoors in the open, but if you decide to overnight in some abandoned farm house or something, beware.

Out in Hawaii they've got centipedes that are big enough to eat birds. Put the serious hurtin' on you. Real boogers. Same deal about outdoors. Won't see 'em. They mostly stay in the brush under rocks and in old wood structures.

Any kind of furry animal you might meet should be considered rabid. Not that they'll go apeshit and attack you like something out of a Stephen King novel or something, but any little nip just might do you in from rabies.

Down South they got lots of cute little raccoons that aren't very afraid of people sometimes. Come right up to you looking for a handout. 'Specially at night if you've got a sammich in the knapsack.

DON'T FUCK WITH THE RACCOONS.

If you're lucky, the only thing that will go wrong will be that your cute furry friend will decide for no apparent reason to bite a 20-stitcher in your ass. If you're not lucky, he'll be rabid. LOTS of wild raccoons have rabies. I have no fucking idea why this is so, but it most surely the hell is. At present there is exactly ONE recorded instance in all of medical history of somebody surviving rabies without getting that happy series of shots in the stomach.

One guy.

Everybody else who tried it died.

And if you get bit and your furry friend runs off into the woods and disappears where they can't check it (by killing it and putting its brains in a blender) to see if it's rabid or not, guess what, it's the shots.

Unless, of course, you want to take your chances on becoming a famous medical celebrity by being the SECOND guy to ever survive.

Rabies makes AIDS seem positively benign.

Bears, coyotes, mountain lions and shit like that go in the same category as tornadoes. If you're destined to have a run in with something like a bear, there's nothing this book can do for you.

Go stand a little farther down the road, would you?

You're crowding me.

Plant Hazards

How 'bout dangerous plants? When's the last time you were attacked by a crazed asparagus? Hopefully, not too recently.

Generally speaking, plants can't really do too much to you unless you go around eating 'em. People who go around eating plants they don't know nuthin' about don't need this book to bail 'em out of trouble. The ones that are still alive might need a shrink maybe, but not this book.

Aside from the annoyances of things like poison ivy and other stuff that can cause you to swell up and scratch like a mongrel dog, there's not much to fear from plants.

Nettles, cactus, sandspurs, thistles and the like are fairly obvious. You go walking around in that kinda stuff and you get the idea pretty quick.

You stay on the road and you're OK. Go off in the damn weeds and... well, you're asking for it. Serves you right.

The only time this doesn't apply is, you guessed it, when overnighting in some strange place you never been before. There's really not too damn much I can tell you that will keep you out of trouble with plants when sleeping in the great outdoors. Stay the hell out of the brush and deep weeds. The heavier the foliage, the more likely it is that there's something in there that's gonna get all over you. Go read the parts about common sense again. As if it's gonna do you any good at all.

Traffic Hazards

Okey-dokey class, will there be any further questions about natural hazards? No? Good. I figure I've about beat that one to death.

Let's turn our workbooks to the part about traffic hazards, then. More fun and games. Wait 'till we get to the part about people hazards. Even better.

Traffic hazards are pretty much covered in the various parts of this text that deal with whatever type of activity that will put you in contact with a given hazard. You know, like fog and stuff like that. Remember what to do when it's foggy? No? Figures. Go back and read it again, then. I don't feel like typing any more.

The bottom line when it comes to traffic hazards is to keep from getting splattered all over the place by the traffic.

Simple enough for you?

There are basically two (well, maybe three) ways to get splattered.

One is to get hit directly by some goof that drifted off the pavement or to be standing ON the pavement and get it (that one serves you right and is Mother Nature's way of culling the infirm and stupid from the hitchhiking herd).

The other way is to get it indirectly from things like people skidding sideways into you after they lost control trying to avoid hitting the fucking dope who didn't pull off the road for you but just stopped right out in the middle of everything.

A bizarre third way to get it is when you have nowhere to jump out of the way of an oncoming idiot. People who hitchhike on elevated roadways with no shoulders and stuff like that deserve every goddamned rotten thing that happens to 'em, and since I hope they all get wiped out sooner instead of later, I'm not gonna try to help 'em out with any little tips and advice in this book.

I feel like I've pretty well covered how to keep from becoming somebody's new hood ornament elsewhere in this book, so I'm not gonna belabor the issue again here.

I'm just as sure as I can be that if there's something obvious that I've missed, somebody's gonna write me a nasty letter telling me how they wouldn't be in their fucking wheelchair for the rest of their life if only I'd had the minimal intelligence to warn them about it here. Tough shit for them but if it's a legitimate item I'll include it in the next edition of this book.

So go tell all your friends to buy one for themselves and another as a gift for that special loved one, so that it'll get reprinted with the latest lifesaving techniques in it. I gotta sell all the ones left over from this edition before the publisher (bless his pointy little head) will crank up the presses again.

Disregarding the callous disregard for life and property expressed in the paragraphs above, there are a few little items you might want to be aware of by way of peculiar traffic hazards and such all.

Like ROAD UNDER CONSTRUCTION for instance.

And sure as hell, one day somebody's gonna let you out of their car right smack in the middle of 10 miles of cement trucks and slopeheads wearing hard hats. Mind what the hell you're doing in a construction area, OK?

God, don't make me remind you guys about common sense again, wouldja?

One little item to be paying attention to in a construction area is debris on the road. This ain't the Navy and they don't have FOD inspection periodically to keep things nice and neat. There's a lotta shit lying around on the road in a construction area. Everything from half-inch washers to sixteen foot pieces of number-32 reinforcing rod. One of those little surprises gets bounced off the surface by car number one and drop-kicked in your direction faster than a Nolan

Ryan fastball by the front end of car (or dump truck) number two, and you're gonna be in for some serious fun.

How good are your reflexes?

How 'bout your hospitalization insurance?

Stay clear of that kind of shit, OK? If a two-by-four drops off a flatbed and ends up right in front of you, then move to somewhere else, fer chrissakes. Somewhere without the little bonus prizes.

Something else to watch for is how much room there is for trucks and stuff to get past you without hitting the barricades on the other side of the pavement. A little constricted area on the road is not a good hitchhiking spot, no matter how many acres there are for people to pull off onto on your side of the pavement.

You ever really take a close look at just how fucking far those rear-view mirrors stick out on the sides of some of those trucks pulling trailers? Just might be a case of reach out and touch someone. And there always always always needs to be room for all the smart people to be able to drive safely around the far side of the dumb sonofabitch who only pulled half way off the pavement to pick you up.

Another good one is where there's a whole bunch of trucks and shit pulling on and off the road up there ahead of you a little ways. Think about visibility. And not just selfishly, as in getting a ride, either.

Whatta you think's gonna happen when some idiot in his useless Trans-Am goes zooming at warp 3 around a low-boy rig pulling a D-8 onto the pavement 50 feet upstream of you with some jerk stopped on the pavement and your worthless ass climbing half inside? WHAM! They'll be cleaning you off the ground in six different places.

One more reason to avoid construction areas is all the shit that falls off of trucks while they're hauling stuff. If you've ever worked construction you'll know exactly what I mean.

Joe Laborer doesn't really give a shit about how much form lumber costs when he's throwing it up on the flatbed to get taken down to the next concrete pour. Doesn't give a shit at all if they lose some along the way. Just toss the suckers up on the truck, and let's go. No tailgate up, no ropes tied around it, no nuthin'. Just bouncing along at 55.

You'll never know what hit you. Seriously. If you survive it, you will not remember even seeing anything. Just all of a sudden waking up in a hospital bed and thinking "Holy shit, what the hell am I doing here?"

I remember once when we were demolishing a launch pad at Cape Canaveral and a piece of steel pipe about four feet long fell off the back of the flatbed and just barely missed the fucking Air Force pad daddy who was driving along behind the truck.

Not maliciously looking for anything, just on his way to a meeting or something. When that son of a bitch came into my office waving that thing around looking for me, I kinda wished it'd hit him square and taken him out. Major fucking hassle.

But do you think the laborers went to any more trouble tying shit down on the truck after that? Fuck no, they thought it was funny. It got to the point where we went along the beach road picking up shit that fell off trucks onto the road shoulders each day, so that the goddamned Air Force wouldn't find it first and jump our shit.

Lotta shit falls off trucks on construction jobs.

Be careful.

One solution to the construction-area problem is to ask to get let out of the car somewhere upstream of all that crap.

Just skip that shit.

People Hazards

And now for the one you've all been waiting for!

People hazards!

Loonies, fags, weirdos, rapists, robbers, cops and all sorts of specimens of humanity who are even worse than a monster living under your bed.

Yes folks, step right up! Read all about it! The very stuff that your mom, your teacher, your preacher, even your boss, said was out there on the road just waiting to get hold of you! Unspeakable terrors of the lonesome roadside! Death and dismemberment that stalks you dressed as a nun! Murder and mayhem that any sane person could have avoided by staying indoors, or calling a taxi. It's all here. Uncensored. Uncut. In all its gruesome detail.

Had enough?

Good.

Now let's get back to the real world, shall we? Your mom and teacher can stay back there reading the tabloids at the supermarket counter. I've got work to do.

Hazards of the road presented by humans (why the hell is it anyway that some folks just WON'T leave you alone?) fall into two easy-to-remember groups. Group number one is the people who are in the cars that stop and pick you up. Group two is everybody else.

Except cops.

They get their own little subsection 'cause they're different.

Pay attention class, there's going to be a quiz on this material sometime next week.

Before I go any further, I'm gonna remind everybody once again to check the figures on what's more dangerous, hitchhiking or walking across the street.

GO LOOK UP THE FUCKING NUMBERS, GODDAMMIT!

You've had it drilled into your head ever since you were old enough to understand what people were saying that hitchhiking was so unspeakably dangerous that the only people who could possibly be out there on the side of the road thumbing for a ride were murderers, too. And when one of the murderers driving a car in search of a tender little boy like you stopped to pick up one of the murderers standing there with their thumb out, a battle to the death was the inevitable result.

Kinda like Godzilla versus Rodan or something.

I can't really blame you. After all, NOBODY has ever bothered to say to your mom, "Hey, wait a minute. How exactly is it that you know hitchhiking is so fearsomely dangerous?" And even if they DID say something like that, your mom would respond by forbidding you to ever hang around with that particular thug again.

Case closed.

In truth, your mom didn't have the faintest idea as to the relative safety of hitchhiking compared with... oh, say climbing up on the roof to get that frisbee you lost.

All your mom had was what the TV newsman told her. And since stories about people falling off of roofs and getting killed don't generate the audience/ad revenue that grisly accounts of a body found in a ditch three states over do, the wise director of the local eyewitless news hour decided to ignore the fell-off-the-roof story, and instead ran as many body-in-the-ditch stories as he could find in the northern hemisphere.

Ditto for people-getting-killed-when-the-radio-fell-in-the-tub-with-them stories. And people-getting-killed-when-they-season-ed-the-shrimp-with-toilet-bowl-cleaner-by-mistake stories. And a whole lotta other stories. The unfortunate victims of these calamities were just as dead, or maimed, as the body in the ditch, and there sure the hell were a lot more of them out there than there were hitchhiking victims, but somehow they weren't as sexy.

Not as titillating.

So, the director of the nightly news acted as if they never happened. After all, Mister Director has a wife and a mortgage to pay for. If the ratings drop, he might be out on the street too. Can't have that.

And so, for that great majority of mindless drones out there across the nation who not only don't bother to get their information somewhere besides the TV, but who also can't even conceive of an information source besides TV, the old lady who slipped on the bathroom floor and died of starvation before the next-door neighbors even noticed they hadn't seen her in two weeks didn't even exist.

But the bodies in the bushes by the interstate kept piling up.

Are we getting the idea here yet? The goddamned brain police who run your local TV station have decided that hitchhiking is deadly dangerous, and in your bovine stupidity (or was it your mom's?), you went right along with the game. GO LOOK UP THE FUCKING NUMBERS, GODDAMMIT!

They're lying there in your public library gathering dust even as I rant.

Your mom lied.

She had no earthly idea what she was talking about when she said to stay off the road, but managed to overpower your better judgment with sheer repetition. Actually, when you think about it, that's quite an accomplishment.

Are we done yet?

Yes.

People Who Stop And Pick You Up

Let's get on with the story.

I'll start out with group number one. The people in the cars who stop and pick you up.

The most dangerous member of this species is the bad driver. You'll get killed ten times over in wrecks caused by the lousy driving of people who pick you up before getting killed once at the hands of people who pick you up.

I have been in cars with people who were such rotten drivers that I was in mortal fear for my life. Most of these people were friends and relatives, but a few had stopped on the roadside to pick me up while I was hitchhiking.

If I had to pick between friends and relatives or total strangers to be scared out of my wits by their driving, I'd pick the strangers every time.

And why, you may ask, would I make such a choice?

Easy.

With the strangers I can say "OK, thanks for the ride. I'm getting out at this corner here," and they stop the car and let me out.

With the friends and relatives, it's no dice. They know in advance just exactly where I'm going, and aren't about to let me out of their deathmobiles.

So if you're ever caught with a maniac driver when hitchhiking, just lie. "Oh, I forgot, I gotta stop here and tell my boss to drop dead." Works every time.

Drunk people can be dangerous when they pick you up. And I'm not talking about drunk drivers, either. Some folks get really belligerent when they're drinking. Just as soon fight you as look at you. Don't argue with the drunk guy who picked you up. Agree with whatever he says.

Most of the time, drunk people are just looking for someone to share their sorry fate with. Go ahead and be a good listener.

Don't egg 'em on or advocate going to their old lady's house to bust her up or anything, though. They just might take you seriously, and you'll wind up in a real jam, duking it out in some sleazy bar with a bunch of crazed ironworkers swinging spud wrenches or something.

I was halfway between Orlando and Miami heading south to my sister's one time when the slobbering drunk guy in the passenger seat

up front pulled out his great big shiny forty-four and started waving it around. I suppose I coulda just panicked and jumped out the window, but instead I stayed put and went along with the flow. Turned out that his buddy who was driving was in bigger trouble than I was. Every time he farted, the guy with the gun threatened to shoot him in the ass.
Really.
You think I make this shit up?
After a while, he even let me hold his shiny toy and admire it. I guess I coulda shot both of 'em if I'd wanted to, but all I wanted was to see Miami before dark, and that's just what I did.
No problem.

Just go with the flow and you'll be alright. Make the weirdo who's got you think you're one of his kind of people. Just another face in the crowd of mutants. Relax and enjoy the ride. To see people like this anywhere else you'd have to pay good money. And if you ever decide to become a writer, you'll definitely be glad you got to make the acquaintance of some of these wackos. They're real good for characterizations and stuff.

A final note about the dingdongs who pick you up. I have to figure you have at least one good eye. Lotsa folks got two. However many eyes you got, USE THEM! As in have a look inside the car BEFORE you get inside. Yes, you really are allowed to do that. It's not considered cheating. Take a gander at them bozos BEFORE you go sitting right next to 'em.
If the guy driving's got a bunch of fag magazines spread out on the front seat (yes, lotsa those kinda folks do just that), chances are pretty good you really didn't want a ride just now after all. Don't

worry about what they'll think when you say "nope" after they crossed three lanes of traffic and squealed rubber just to stop. Fuck 'em!

Weird-looking crazies that even the Hell's Angels wouldn't let inside the clubhouse? Forget it!

What can they do to you? You're out in public where the whole world can see, so they really don't want to start a fight.

YOU are the one who makes the decision. Nobody else. Never forget that you are the one in control of who may and who may not give you a ride.

People Out On The Streets With You

Now for everybody else. All those people out there on the streets. Except the cops. Like before in the part about traffic hazards, I'm gonna remind you that I've already covered most of this kinda stuff in other parts of the book that detail this or that activity which could put you in touch with the bad guys out on the street.

Really, all that knowing about the hazards posed by all those people out there on the street with you boils down to is just common-sense burglarproofing your personal self. The same shit you'd do to avoid getting mugged when going around the corner to the local beer store.

Take note that the bad guys in the baddest part of town don't go around mugging each other. They go after the overdressed weenies with the double extra-fat wallet bulge in their J.C. Penney's slacks.

Just don't look like an easy mark.

And never carry around more than you can afford to lose. This is so damn easy that nobody does it. Too simple.

Who you trying to impress out there, anyway? Forget it.

If you're out on the road thumbing, you're invisible. Just another pair of jeans and a T-shirt.

If you're in street-gang country, take note of the colors that the gangs wear, and wear something else so as to avoid a random drive-by shooting or something equally cheerful.

Oughtta be good close-ups on the local news at six o'clock that you can study for what the boyz are wearing this fashion season. Gang violence is almost as sexy as a body on the interstate, and the news director can't get enough of it.

I'm presuming that you aren't planning on hitchhiking to or through street-gang land on a regular basis. If you are, you already know all about how to conduct yourself on the streets, and this book ain't got a damn thing in it that you don't already know.

If some joker with a large knife and small IQ comes up to you to take your dollar eighty-seven, go ahead and let him. He probably needs it more than you, anyway.

Be gracious about it. If it's more than you can afford to lose, tough shit, I told you not to carry that much. You shoulda sewed it into the lining of your underwear or something like that.

If you're gonna ignore what I'm telling you here, then you deserve it. You sure the hell can't go around whining that nobody ever tried to tell you.

Let's go talk about the cops, I'm tired of all this other shit.

Cops

An unavoidable fact of life in hitchhiking, as well as everything else for that matter, is the cops.

Period.

Now the fact that cops are unavoidable is by no means the same thing as saying that the cops are by definition a bunch of rotten sonofabitches.

Not at all.

I'm presuming that while you're sitting there reading this book you've got a picture already in your mind of the cops as some sort of horrible monsters. If I'm wrong and you don't, well alright! Good for you. Go ahead and skip this chapter as a reward for such a good attitude. You probably won't need any of the stuff that's in it anyway.

Now, as for the rest of you guys, listen up! I'll say this in one short sentence so as you can't go whining to somebody later on that nobody ever told you, and then I'll go on for the rest of this section to explain how what I'm about to say works. OK?

EVERYTHING CRUMMY THAT THE COPS HAVE EVER DONE TO YOU OR ANY OF YOUR FRIENDS IS 'CAUSE OF YOUR OWN DAMN FAULT!

There, didja get that? If not, read it again until you do.

Let's be realistic here. The cops are composed entirely of human beings. Really. And just like every other variety of human being you've encountered in your life, they're gonna shit on you if you piss them off.

The main difference is that the cops are far better prepared than anybody else on Earth (including the Iranians) to shit all over you right this second when you piss them off.

DON'T PISS OFF THE COPS!

There, didja get that? If not, read it again until you do.

Whether or not you like it, the cops like it, or even God likes it, those wonderful folks who go by the name "politicians" in mixed company and who also just happen to be the ones who make our laws have really gone out of their collective ways to make some real dandy legal statutes. And chances are that when a cop stops to have a little roadside chat with you, it's on account of 'cause somewhere along the line you are in violation of one of those dandy legal statutes.

Whether or not you like it or even understand it. I mean come on, the cops are a lot like everybody else; why would they want to take the trouble to stop to deal with some dirtbag hitchhiker when they could otherwise just keep on cruising down the road in that really neat-o fast car with all the nifty doodads in it?

It's 'cause the city fathers want to keep their roads clear of all those hitchhiking scumbuckets (that's you and me, can't forget where we really stand in the great scheme of things, can we?), and if the cops aren't out there doing their job, then somebody's gonna complain and who knows, maybe they'll get kicked off the force for not doing their job or something.

The only possible exception to this being the one and only reason for a cop ever stopping to talk to you is maybe cause he's a fag or something and he's trying to pick you up cause you got a nice butt.

For now, we'll assume that all cops are full-tilt heterosexuals whose only use for the gay element of the population is something to swat with a nightstick.

So. There you sit/stand with a cop car parked right next to you on the side of the road (you can forget getting a ride for the duration of the cop's visit), and a great big cop getting out of it. Whatta you do?

It's more a matter of what you don't do.

Keep right up front there in the center of your consciousness the fact that before you even open up your mouth to say hello to the cop, you've got two strikes against you.

Strike one is that you are very likely breaking some kinda law somehow (and it's not for you to know which one it is or how you're breaking it, that's the cop's job). Strike two is that you have interrupted the cop's thoroughly enjoyable cruise down the highway with your mindless violation of the law, so he's probably in a bad mood as a result.

DO NOT: Make any sudden moves (you just might be an exact match for the description of that very armed-and-dangerous bank robber who killed three people down at the second-to-last national that just came in over the radio).

DO NOT: Try to convince the cop that he doesn't know what the hell he's doing and that you haven't done anything wrong.

DO NOT: Tell the cop that you've got constitutional rights.

DO NOT: Say ANYTHING in a tone of voice that expresses anything other than a sincere regard for the unappreciated difficulties of being a cop.

DO NOT: Play dumb.

DO NOT: Refuse to comply with ANY request or demand the cop makes (short of "gimme a blow job").

DO NOT: Allow yourself to appear to the cop (remember, HIS PERCEPTION, not yours) as a difficult bastard to deal with.

DO NOT: Argue with the cop.

DO NOT: Be carrying ANY booze, drugs or stolen property (or even anything that might be mistaken for booze, drugs or stolen property).

DO NOT: Be drunk or stoned out of your mind on something.

DO NOT: Be in a hurry and act impatient.

DO NOT: Try to leave before the cop lets you.

DO NOT: Rise to any bait the cop may taunt you with.

DO NOT: Tell the cop about all your problems and how bad you got it.

Have you got the idea here yet? Be nice, will you! The nicer you are, the nicer the cop's gonna be. Trust me on this one. OK?

DO: Use a nice friendly tone of voice when talking to the cop.

DO: Answer all the questions the cop might ask you. Promptly. Intelligently.

DO: Be honest.

DO: Try to make the cop's job a little easier if you can.

DO: Be understanding.

DO: Engage the cop in friendly conversation if he seems inclined that way.

DO: Take your time and bear with it while the cop writes stuff down in his little book or goes back into his car for who the hell knows what.

DO: Stay put until the cop specifically says "OK, you can go now."

DO: Apologize for causing the cop any trouble by making him have to stop and check you out (but you better be sincere and convincing, or otherwise he's gonna think you're a real smart-ass and nail you).

DO: Accept with kind equanimity (go look it up) all racial slurs, smart remarks, taunts, provocations and physical contact that the cop may dish out.

DO: Cooperate with the cop.

DO: Cheerfully admit to having made a mistake in breaking whatever law it was that caused the cop to accost you in the first place (including laws you never heard of or don't believe in).

DO: Admit to having had a couple if you've had a couple (there's no law against having a little alcohol in your system as long as you're not making a public nuisance of yourself).

Look, here's the deal. This ain't some kind of exam you have to study for. I already know there's no way you can remember all this stuff. So don't worry about it.

The main thing, is you gotta apply a liberal dose of common sense (which ain't none too common now, is it?) to situations involving yourself and the cops.

Look at it from the cop's point of view. Can you imagine all the horseshit stories and excuses that any cop who's been on the job for more than... oh, say a week... has heard?

Yeah.

So don't even bother. You can't possibly think up some story that the cop's just gonna sit there and take without a peep. Don't even try.

Not only that but after a while cops acquire a sixth sense about people. They can SMELL bullshit. And all that does is piss them off, 'cause they know you're trying to put one over on 'em.

DON'T PISS OFF THE COPS, dammit.

How many times I gotta tell you that, anyway?

Actually, the fact that all the cops ever get from people day after day all day long on the job is hostility and lies is really an advantage.

Think about it.

People respond to kindness, right? So just imagine the response to kindness that somebody who never sees kindness is gonna come across with.

Yeah. That's it.

Now I'm not saying that every cop you see is gonna roll over and play dead every time you say please and thank you. As in any other group of people you could pick, there's always going to be a few certified assholes that have a case of the permanent red ass for everything they encounter, including you at your charming best.

There's nothing you can do to improve your lot with these types. But think about it. There's probably plenty of stuff you could do to make things worse!

Being hauled down to the station house for fingerprinting and the whole wazoo ain't nearly as bad as having the living hell clubbed out of you and then going down to the stationhouse, now is it?

I didn't think so either.

So lighten up.

Chances are pretty good that the result of your little roadside chat is gonna be a request from the cop that you take a walk to remove yourself from whatever less-than-legal area you are presently occupying.

DO IT!

The cop doesn't really want to be bothered with having to process your worthless ass, and you sure the hell don't want to get processed. By virtue of the fact that you're out on the road thumbing in the first place, I'm gonna assume that you've got lotsa time on your hands. You can cover 3 miles in a single hour of relaxed walking unless you're carrying a piano or something, and you are certainly healthy enough to take the walk (otherwise you wouldn't be out here in the first place). All this stuff screams, "Go ahead and take the walk!"

Don't take it personally. Just remove your presence from the area. How hard is it, anyway?

And don't try anything smart-o like trudging along 'till the cop rounds the first corner and disappears, and then turning back to face traffic with your thumb out.

That's dumb.

Either the original cop or one of his buddies is gonna be back by to check on you every so often. If the cop said to go to at least "so-and-so" then go to so-and-so. If he didn't, then use your head and get your ass to some kind of place that bears little or no resemblance to the one you got pinched at in the first place.

Chances are, you were on the expressway (I told you not to hitchhike there), standing there like a goof right under the sign that says "LIMITED ACCESS TOLLWAY, PEDESTRIANS AND VEHICLES UNDER 5 BRAKE HORSEPOWER PROHIBITED," so quit whining and get over to that on-ramp I told you about.

When you stop to think about it, you really have to work extra hard at it to get busted for real when hitchhiking.

The only time in my life that I ever got busted hitchhiking was when I started out by thumbing while sitting(!) on the pavement(!) and then forced the cop to arrest me (he was only trying to keep me from killing myself by getting run over by some dazed tourist down in Florida) by giving him a lotta horseshit in a loud voice, and then followed that by slamming the door to the cop shop as hard as I could.

Brilliant, huh?

Net result: half a day in the local pokey and $136.00 in fines. The whole thing was ENTIRELY my own fault. Nobody else's. If I'd had the minimal intelligence required to NOT PISS OFF THE COPS and just moved on down the road when asked to, nothing would have happened and the only thing I'd have lost would have been this story of unbridled stupidity.

I could do without the story.

For a while, one of the local municipalities in Florida enacted a law banning hitchhiking altogether. This little town just happened to be right in the middle of the 30-mile stretch that I hitchhiked daily going to and from my job as a janitor for over a year ('till I moved a little closer to work, and then only had to thumb 10 miles there and back). And as anybody who's lived there can verify, small-town cops in the South can be a real pain in the ass. Nothing to trifle with.

So did I quit my job or risk getting thrown in jail daily?

Hell no, I merely took the trouble when asking people that had just picked me up how far they were going, and requested that if they weren't going all the way through Friendlyville to please drop me off at some really good corner for hitchhiking of my choosing somewhere upstream of the city-limit sign.

No problem.

Every car that stopped for me at that corner got the same question, and if they weren't going all the way through town, then I didn't get in.

No problem.

Nobody ever got upset at me for not getting in after they'd taken the trouble to stop for me, and lotsa times people would go out of their way in order to take me all the way through town.

Never in that whole year of daily hitchhiking through that place did I get stranded in town and have to deal with their cops.

Not once.

So don't start whining about how bad it is, OK? A little forethought and intelligence on your part, and every experience you have with the cops will be a pleasant one. Sometimes they'll even give you a ride to where you're going.

I know 'cause I've done it.

Part Four:
Advanced Techniques
And Sneaky Tricks

OK, here comes the good part. The part where you learn some of the sneaky tricks and advanced techniques that the pros use.

All's fair in love, war and hitchhiking.

Since you've read and understood all the stuff in here (you HAVE, haven't you?) up to this point, I can safely presume that you're ready to climb one rung higher on the hitchhiking ladder and area now smart enough to hang on to the ladder and not fall off.

I make the last statement on account of 'cause if the stuff I'm about to tell you isn't done just so, it'll backfire on you as often as not.

Keep in mind, however, that what you're about to read isn't the end-all and be-all of advanced hitchhiking. There are as many sly ways to improve your odds as there are sly people out there thumbing. Think of this section as a stimulus to your own creativity instead of some kind of set of rules that can never be bent or broken. If you come up with a good one, write me a letter describing it and I'll share it with your fellow hitchhikers in the next edition of this book.

Time to polish up the old stage presence. The show must go on.

Props

The main thing we'll cover here will be props. Yes, props.

Just like on stage. Hitchhiking props come in all shapes and sizes, from scraps of cloth to other people. The only thing they really have in common is the use they'll be put to.

Getting you a ride. Sooner.

Physical artifacts that can be used as hitchhiking props are a world unto themselves. Some are just lying around to be used as found, and others involve time, money, and even considerable work in their production.

The only guide to whether or not a prop is worth it is: "Is it more trouble to drag around (and maybe risk getting stolen) than it's worth for snagging rides?" If it's clunky, bothersome to carry around, and not earning its keep, get rid of it.

The sooner the better.

We'll start with something that's just lying around out there on the side of the road. Sometimes. Parked or abandoned cars. Don't laugh, there's more of 'em than you might think.

If you're getting close to where your ride's gotta drop you off (you already asked where, of course, as soon as you got inside the car), you might want to be on the lookout for any cars parked on the shoulder of the road and ask to be let off nearby one. Or, if you forgot about that, you might want to have a look around at wherever it is you happen to be standing to see if there are any parked cars. No, not parked legally in an official parking spot, but just kinda off to the side of the road. Looking like maybe they ran out of gas or something (this doesn't work too good in town where all the cars look parked).

However you come on it, go plant yourself right next to the dead car like it belongs to you. That is, as long as it's in a safe spot for folks to get on and off the road. That's it, stand right there and try to look like a stranded motorist.

People who would NEVER stop for a hitchhiker will gladly take a stranded motorist almost anywhere. It's probably not a good idea to tell them it's not your car after they've picked you up. They might not see the humor in it, and drop you off right now. In a terrible hitchhiking spot. Just play along and everything will be Hunky dory. Maybe tell 'em you locked the keys inside. They just MAY take you all the way to where you're going. Right to the doorstep. Where your spare set of keys is.

Be sure to say, "Thank you."

Aside from cars, there's not too damn much lying around out there in the great out-of-doors that you can use as a prop.

Too bad.

So let's look around the house for some stuff, OK? Remember that really neat sign (which, technically speaking, is also a prop) we made out of the paper plate? Hard to believe how good that sucker worked, huh?

Hmm... let's see here; how 'bout that set of crutches collecting dust in the back of the closet? The ones you had to walk on after you tried to take that turn into your driveway all the way from the TOP of Death Hill on your skateboard? Yeah, those. Try that. People are suckers for a pitiful person in need. And besides, even the most callous bastards can't tell themselves, "let the sonofabitch walk" as they whiz past you standing there hanging over your crutches.

Just don't RUN up to the car that stopped for you, OK? Make it look good. Tell 'em you're on your way home from the orthopedist's office. Something believable. Maybe wrap an Ace bandage around your ankle.

Military uniforms are good, too. Even if you got thrown out of the Army for stealing the general's Hum-Vee. Who's gonna ever know about that as long as you don't tell 'em? Back in the '70s it was a different story, but nowadays a nice crisp uniform can work wonders.

Another great item is a motorcycle helmet. Or even a football helmet. Most states have helmet laws, and if you don't have one, you're gonna get busted when you're riding a cycle. I couldn't tell you how many times guys riding cycles have pointed to their heads, shrugged, and sailed on past me. People on bikes tend to be more inclined to give hitchhikers rides than everybody else. Why, I don't know. But it's true. So pack a helmet and be sure to hang on tight.

OK. Let's move on to even sneakier stuff. Stuff that isn't what it appears to be. Like the old 5-gallon gas can that's not a gas can. This routine is so old, it's new. Lotsa people laugh when you mention it. Like it's too hokey to even dignify by acknowledgment. Wrong! This little ploy really works. Folks on the road back in the '30s were using this one to get around.

People see you on the side of the road with a gas can and they stop. No need to be next to either a car or a gas station. Out in the middle of nowhere is just fine. I know folks who have cleverly put a false bottom in one of these and then poured a spot of gas over the top of that. Great for convincing thieves that there's nothing in there. Really. And then pour some out. See?

About the only problem with the fake gas can is that it's a great big clunky piece of shit you gotta drag around all over the place. For that reason it's not really too good of an idea for in-town thumbing. Much better for cross-country where you've gotta carry some extra shit with you anyway.

However, a one-gallon can with nothing in it at all is easy enough to handle, and will work wonders in town or anywhere else for that matter.

Just make sure it's one of those fire-engine red numbers with the word GAS or FLAMMABLE on it in foot-high letters so that even the idiots whooshing by in Porsches and Corvettes can recognize it.

Another neat thing about gas cans is that they're one of the only ploys that don't piss everybody off when you tell 'em, "No, I'm not out of gas, this was just to get your attention," or something like that. Everybody I've ever encountered this way was not only *not* pissed for being faked out, but instead seemed to admire my creativity. Your luck with people may be different than mine, though, so don't go rubbing it in.

When in doubt, don't give the secret away. Keep it to yourself.

You like that?
There's more.

Wrapping an arm or leg in white rags that you've dyed to look bloody is a real traffic-stopper too. Mind the color. Blood isn't exactly a regular red when it dries. It's darker. And kinda brownish, too.

This one also involves some acting on your part. And some scripting, too. Have whoever picks you up take you to that hospital that's only a block away from where you're going. And act like it hurts the whole time you're in the car.

People WILL get pissed off over this one if you let 'em know it's a hoax. Don't like it at all if they find out you've duped 'em. Be sure and have your story ready before you go out on the street in one of these rigs, too.

There's a world of other stuff laying around that can be pressed into service as a hitchhiking prop but I'm not gonna go on and on about it. Different circumstances demand different solutions. Use your brains. If you're smart enough to travel cross-country for free, then it's not too much more to ask that you think up some clever props to satisfy your own particular needs.

One last word about props.

Don't go using 'em over and over.

People get wise real fast. Even the ones who never stop to pick you up.

I mean, how many times do YOU gotta see the same guy with a gas can thumbing before you decide something's fishy?

Miscellaneous Dodges

Here's a little tidbit that I don't know where else to put, so I'm gonna drop it in right here.

Ignore every last one of those "No Riders" signs. The boss puts those on the car, or truck, and once his employee (the driver) gets around the first corner it's a whole different deal. I've gotten zillions of rides in cars and trucks that had "No Riders" stickers plastered all over 'em. Screw the boss.

Something else to be mindful of is ways of catching people's eyes. Stand out in a crowd and all that kinda stuff.

There's ways to do that, too.

Let's suppose you're on a one-way road. What happens if you get on the "wrong" side of the pavement? You will sure the hell have their attention. It feels weird at first standing there with the wrong arm out but you'll get used to it pretty quick.

This is also a good one for nighttime thumbing. Sometimes it turns out that the very best visibility spot is over on the "wrong" side of the road. If it's one way, there IS no wrong side.

Sometimes the best spot to pull off the road onto is over there on the "wrong" side. Have considerations like that floating around in the back of your mind all the time, so that when an appropriate situation comes up, you'll know what to do right away.

Clothing can fit into this department of dirty tricks, too. But the line between an outfit that catches their eyes and an outfit that repels them is an awfully thin one. This sort of thing requires a little trial and error. Every area of the country is different, so what works in Berkeley is likely to bomb in Birmingham.

Let your behavior or whatever fit the situation.

Be flexible. Be ready to do it the "wrong" way.

Part Five:
Anecdotes, War Stories,
And Other Loose Ends

This is the part of the book where the stuff that didn't quite fit in anywhere else goes. It all relates directly to hitchhiking, but it's not really relevant to the well-defined parts of the book you've already read. So I just kinda lumped it all here in this last part of the book.

Getting Laid

Yep, you can run into the damndest things out there on the road. Including good-looking girls who want to get inside your pants. Of course, these days, you better be careful. Might get something on you that won't wash off.

Before we go any further here, I want to make it clear that I'm NOT talking prostitutes here. No whores.

Just friendly people who want to have a little exotic fun.

My personal experience with getting a little on the side while hitchhiking extends to several separate nubile young women, both directly (as in jumping in the sack the same day you first set eyes on them) and indirectly (as in swapping a phone number or having them coming back by unexpectedly to your house after they've dropped you off there) over the course of time.

Some were a one-shot deal and others became long-term friends and lovers. One of the neat things about getting laid when hitchhiking is that both parties have zero illusions about any romantic horseshit. I mean, there's no doubt at all as to the nature of the relationship. As long as you're fun, I'll keep coming around; you quit being fun, I quit coming by.

What could be more straightforward and to the point? None of this dinner-and-dancing shit. None of the weird indirect crap that a lot of folks love to indulge in.

I suppose that if you're a sappy type who thinks a proper relationship ought to have a little more to it than an occasional romp in the hay, you're not gonna do very well on return engagements. You won't be any fun. You're taking it too seriously.

You can get laid hitchhiking two different ways. One is to have a lusty lady pull over and let you in. The other is to MEET somebody else hitchhiking. Of the two, getting picked up by the person you're gonna be romping with in short order is by far the most likely.

One time I got picked up by a guy driving a Corvette with a good looking blonde in the passenger seat, and she told me to sit on her lap. It was HER car and she was just letting this guy have a little fun by letting him drive it around some.

She got to squirming around and it was pretty obvious what was gonna happen next. They took me back to her house on the ocean and there was ANOTHER girl there with the hots. I was on my way to work, and already late, so I couldn't stick around for round two. Hell of a job of self-control, huh?

Anyway, about a month later, in the middle of the night, here comes a little white Volkswagen beetle and pulls off to let me in. Once again there was a guy driving, and this time there was a brunette in the passenger seat. Turns out that the brunette was the other one in that blonde's house that day! And she was ready to go! Whee! This is fun! Let's make up for lost time! The only bad part about the whole deal was the look on that guy's face when she said I could spend the night but he had to go home. Too bad! I felt sorry for him.

Once in Hawaii I got let out at a corner where there was this girl thumbing who was already there waiting for a lift. One thing led to another, and after we got picked up she decided to stop off where I was staying for the time being in a place called Punaluu, and we wound up getting it on inside an honest-to-God Hawaiian grass shack. Built by an honest-to-God Hawaiian way back when. Just like something out of one of those hokey South Pacific movies or something. After play time was over she got back out on the road and headed to wherever the hell she was going and disappeared forever.

See ya.

The point of all this story-telling is to illustrate that, yes, it really DOES happen. Forget planning on anything as far off the wall as getting a piece of ass when hitchhiking. There's no way in hell it's gonna work. It's just one of those little bonus items that comes along whenever the hell it feels like it, and that's all there is to it.

Just be careful and don't go getting AIDS or something, OK?

Hitchhiking For Women

OK, since we're sorta on the subject here I may as well take the time to detail the particulars of hitchhiking for women.

This whole book is aimed at a male audience. That's for a reason. Most hitchhikers are guys. By an overwhelming majority, I might add. So turn the page and we'll do hitchhiking for women, OK?

DO NOT!

Didja get that? If not, read it again until you do.

I'm not kidding. This is the one aspect of hitchhiking where the odds of getting in over your head aren't so infinitesimal. There's just too fucking many assholes out there who have this weird idea in their heads that if a girl's out thumbing, then she's asking for it. Why they think this I have no idea, but it's unfortunately a common perception among the less-intelligent segment of the male species. Say about 90 percent of 'em.

I suppose if you MUST hitchhike, ladies, you may as well plan on something really weird happening sooner or later. Probably sooner. Every damn woman I know that used to hitchhike quit after somebody went bonkers on 'em. Notice how I say USED TO HITCHHIKE. I don't know any girl right now who hitchhikes on a regular basis.

Not one.

Same shit goes for giving people rides, too.

Drugs And Hitchhiking

OK, now we've covered THAT cheerful subject let's go on to another real smiler.

DRUGS.

Yuck. Drugs. No fun allowed. Taking drugs with you on the road ain't too fucking smart, now is it? Hell, taking drugs *period* ain't too smart either, is it? How long before a cop stops to check you out and just happens to have one of them dogs with him? Or maybe you start acting squirrely and he searches you? Sooner or later, the odds are gonna catch up with you.

Another very good reason to avoid drugs when hitchhiking is to minimize the chances of getting knocked over the head and losing all those nice rocks, or pills, or whatever you're in possession of. Never mind getting hit hard enough to where you don't wake back up. Or getting pushed out of the car a couple of quarts low on blood.

I suppose that if you're doing drugs right now on a regular basis it probably means you're not gonna listen to this. You don't listen very good to anything, do you? Whatever.

Anyhow, you can't say I didn't tell you.

Needless to say, if somebody that picks you up offers you some of what's going around and you accept, you're on your own. Nothing I can do or say that's gonna do you a bit of good. It's strictly a pass-or-fail test.

Being In Somebody's Car When They Get Busted

While we're talking about people getting nailed by the cops and stuff, I'm gonna ask you a question I bet you never thought of: What the hell do you do if the person who gave you a ride gets pulled over and busted?

Good question, huh?

Actually, it's not such a big deal. Relax. It's a lot like the part about YOU getting busted by the cops. It's more what you DON'T do that makes a difference. Don't freak out and panic. Take it easy, nothing's gonna happen to you. You didn't break any law, did you? No? Good, everything's gonna be just fine.

About the only way to get into serious trouble is if the guy robbed a bank or something while you were in the car. That makes you an accessory to the crime. Not a good idea. Also about as likely as getting killed by having a meteorite hit you on the head while you're walking down the street.

Just don't be in a hurry and try to bolt out of there without asking the cop if it's OK. He's gonna have to check you out first, so it might be a while while he processes the dorf who picked you up. When he's done, you can go. If you check out OK, that is. Another good reason to be squeaky clean while out in the wide, wonderful world. Otherwise, you might be late getting to where you were going.

Like five to twenty years or so.

Roadside Etiquette
With Other Hitchhikers

Suppose, for instance, someone drops you off at a corner where there's already somebody else there thumbing. Maybe five or six somebodies.

Whatta you do?

This happens a lot more often than you might think, so it's worth considering.

What you oughtta do winds up looking like the purest of pure altruism, but it's not. You get behind the guy who's FARTHEST from the corner (this always happens at intersections) and wait your turn. It enhances your odds of getting a ride soonest.

Allow me to explain how this works.

If you'll notice, when there's more than one guy on the corner, they're usually spaced apart from each other. And not just ten feet or so, either. Generally there's enough room between people for a car to stop and then pull back out after picking up just one guy. This is for a reason. Two reasons, actually.

Those of us who do a lot of this sort of thing know that the guy closest to the corner is most likely to get a ride. Before everybody else. Once he's gone everybody moves up one place in line. So why be a nice guy and stand back at the end?

Good question.

Reason number one is very direct and honest. You go jumping some guy in the line and he just might get pissed off, come up behind you, and knock the living shit out of you. Nobody likes a ripoff, and that's exactly what you're doing when you jump somebody in the line.

If some idiot is hanging back there a hundred yards from the corner, don't sweat it. Otherwise, ask nicely before getting closer to the intersection than somebody who's already there.

Also, do not just assume that if you get dropped off right next to somebody there at the corner that it's OK to stay there right next to him. It's not. He doesn't want you there. Go away.

That's the obvious reason. Pissing somebody off. Probably why 95 percent of hitchhikers do it. But there's another reason too.

A sneaky mathematical reason.

As in, "mathematical odds of getting the hell out of there as soon as possible."

People who will stop and give one person a lift won't stop and give two or more people a lift. Don't ask why. Just is.

Maybe they think they can take one guy if he starts something, but not two guys. It doesn't matter why. Just is.

Never mind. Here's the bottom line.

Two separate people hitchhiking the same place one after the other can BOTH get rides and be gone quicker than both of 'em hitchhiking together will. Understand that?

At first, it doesn't seem like that could possibly be the case, but it is. And if you think about it a little, it's not so crazy. However long it takes you to get a ride by yourself in a particular spot, it's gonna take more than TWICE that long if you're hitchhiking with an extra person. You gotta play the odds when you're thumbing, and those are the odds. And it gets even worse the more people you've got with you. Much worse.

Don't believe me? No problem. Just do what I did. Wear a watch and start timing things. This little experiment works really good if you're thumbing to work and back every day.

You're gonna be in the same places, at the same times, every day, for a whole bunch of days. Same conditions every time. Same odds of getting a ride every time. It adds up after a while, and just like when you're throwing dice or playing poker, all the variations are gonna smooth out and the actual odds of getting a ride are gonna be all that's left.

Takes longer with two (or more) together than it takes for each separately.

And there's even a sneak back-door for when some three hundred pound gorilla with an attitude steps in front of you. Don't even bother to get upset. Just slide on down the road away from the gorilla a decent distance and thumb by yourself.

Incredibly, people can sense that the guy who japped you is an asshole and they'll sail right past him to stop for you. Not always, but a hell of a lot more times than you'd ever imagine possible without going out on the streets and trying this stuff over and over.

No shit. People like that usually have a look on their faces, and we all know about your expression and how it affects your chances, don't we? I'm not promising this will happen EVERY time (remember, we're playing percentages here), but it'll happen often enough to keep you smiling.

Be sure to grin at the creep through the back window as you pull out into the traffic.

One more little tidbit and we'll go on to something else. If you're in line behind somebody and a car stops to let them in, don't go running up to the car as if they gotta let you in too. They don't. And if you act like they owe you something, they're gonna give you a look and drive off without you.

Better by far to just stand there where you're at and give 'em one of those faces I've talked about earlier in this thing. You don't know if the guy who stopped was the brother-in-law of whoever was out there in front of you or not. Somebody who NEVER gives strangers rides. So don't act pushy or forward. Won't work. Just look sad and forlorn and lonesome. They'll feel sorry for you, and after you've made solid eye contact with the driver he'll take pity on you and give you the nod.

So that's how that works.

If They're Gonna Kill You, You Might As Well...

Next topic.

If they're gonna kill you, you might as well... what?

Another good question.

Before we do any more of this one, I have a confession to make. I don't have the faintest idea about what I'm fixing to talk about here. Not only have I never been in any kind of situation like this, I've never in my life met or talked to anybody else who's been in some kind of a jam like this.

So fair warning, I'm making it up as I go along.

I have, however, given this one a little thought, and this is what I've decided that I would do if presented with some kind of nightmare situation like this. I've got it divided into two separate courses of action. Both of which I am assuming put me inside a moving car with some bloodthirsty homicidal maniacs. I mean, if you're not in the car, how are they gonna get you? Right?

Well, I guess they could run over you, so be alert. But that should go without saying .

So anyhow, we're in the car with an armed loony and that's the position we're gonna proceed from. OK?

If you can think of some way something like the scenarios I'm gonna describe can happen while you're outside the car, drop me a line so I can put it in the next edition of this thing. And don't give me any shit about how they can pull over, stick a gun in your face, and MAKE you get inside the car with them. That kind of shit only happens in Iran and Lebanon and cheerful places like that. Somebody pulls something like that on me here in America and I already KNOW they're gonna do me in if I get in the car with them. So I got absolutely NOTHING TO LOSE by turning around and running for it.

One more thing before we start here. Make damn sure that what they want to do with you is the worst. You go trying this stuff and you're going to get hurt. Not killed, but you might get hurt pretty bad. Well, come to think of it, you might possibly get killed doing this. But the odds arc dcfinitcly in your favor. So, without going so far out of your way as to refuse to believe that they mean you serious harm or worse, be extra damn sure about the situation you really are in.

Like you say "I want out," and they say no, and then they start going somewhere you don't want to go. Like some little dirt road off into the woods or something. Shit like that. If it ever happens (less likely than your odds of becoming a big movie star or a professional football player), you'll know.

Course of action number one is "Get the hell out of here. NOW!" Although it's gonna put a serious road rash all over you, you CAN jump from a moving car. Even a very fast-moving one. Like on the freeway doing 95. Don't believe me? Go talk to one of your friends who's been riding a motorbike for years and years.

People who ride motorbikes a lot usually have experience with zooming down the road at high speed without benefit of something to be riding on. They call it "laying the bike down." Sounds innocent enough all right, but it's a real adventure. Some of 'em are lucky and they come out of it with maybe a scratch on their arm or something. Some of 'em aren't as lucky and get into the hospital for a while. None of 'em get killed, though. Unless they get run over by that cement truck that was right behind 'em, or maybe they laid it down when they missed a turn in front of a bunch of trees or telephone poles. And if you jump out of a car, you don't have to worry about getting the living shit pounded out of you by a low-flying motorcycle.

Pick your time with care. It makes a difference. Stopped at a traffic light is the very best. Taking a turn at an intersection is good too. They gotta go slow or they'll wreck.

Fun subject, huh?

Also, the more people there are around, the better. Not so much because they're gonna come rescue you. Far from it, they'll all probably just pretend nothing's happening. But if you go jumping out of a car and there're folks around watching, the bad guys are much less likely to stop and come back for you.

Course of action number two is "Derail the train." Grab the fucking steering wheel and give it a good yank. That will DEFINITELY occupy the attention of every single occupant of the car. ALL OF 'EM. They'll forget all about the terrible stuff they were planning on doing to you. If you can manage to wreck the car, they won't want to play any more. They'll be too busy with personal problems to be messing with you.

And if they shoot at you when you grab the wheel, so what? The car's gonna be bouncing all over the place, and they won't have good aim. Even from two feet away. And they only get one shot anyhow before all of you pile into the ditch upside down. Hell, if there's more than one of 'em, they're just as likely to shoot each other as shoot you when the car starts going out of control. Many gunshot wounds do not result in death. Most people who die 'cause somebody shot 'em got hit with a multitude of slugs. Ditto for knife wounds. The guy's only got one go at you before the car's rolling over and over down the shoulder of the road.

Yes, the crash might kill you. Unlikely as hell, but it might. But I thought we'd already decided you were gonna get killed anyway. Remember? So what have you got to lose?

This is a waste of time. None of this is ever gonna happen.

When To Say "Fuck It" And Start Walking

Onwards and upwards.

How 'bout when should you say, "Fuck this shit!" and just start hoofing it?

How fast can you walk?

How tired are you? How far you gotta go?

What time is it?

How many cars are on the road?

What kind of place is it and how likely are ANY of those bastards to stop?

All this and more comes into the decision to quit thumbing and start walking.

As a really good way of looking at this one, I just compare whether or not it's gonna take me longer to walk to where I'm going than it's gonna take me to get a ride. If the walk looks like it's gonna take longer, I just keep thumbing.

This, of course, takes experience. Which I presume you ain't got too much of, or otherwise howcum you're reading this?

Generally speaking, people cover about three miles in an hour of steady walking. No jogging. None of that Olympic walking, either. Just a nice regular pace.

So. If you're out in the middle of nowhere late at night and it looks like you'll be doing good if you get a ride in the next hour, start walking if you're less than THREE MILES from where you're going. That's a long ways.

Let's say you're in a really good spot and the traffic flow is just right on a Saturday afternoon. On average, you should expect to get a ride within fifteen minutes or so. How close should you be before you start with the legs? Well... let's see here. Fifteen minutes is one quarter of an hour, and if you can travel three miles walking in that one hour then you'll be able to cover one quarter of three miles in fifteen minutes.

Over half a mile.

Damn! That don't seem right. Half mile's a pretty good throw.

However, despite the fact that liars figure, these figures don't lie. This ain't the whole story, though.

I'm lazy. It's a lot easier to stand by the road than it is to take a hike. So for myself, I generally don't give up until I'm a little less than a half mile. Not too much less, though. Unless I've gotta be there on time. Gotta play those odds.

One thing to be aware of is how short of a distance is so short it pisses off the guy who gave you a ride. You know, like he stops, and then you say, "Right here's fine," before he even gets into third gear. Not a good idea. Once you've done that, you can forget getting a ride from that guy ever again. Needless to say, that ain't so smart when you're thumbing around town. It's the same people on that road day after day. Don't want to waste any of 'em.

If you're in that "it's just starting to rain but nothing's wet yet" deal we talked about before, short hops are OK. The amount of time you can normally expect to wait drops way off, and in that little bit of time (on average, don't forget this is all averages) you can't walk very far.

If you're out on the lonesome road to nowhere with one car coming past you about every fifteen minutes, make sure you don't fall into the "thumb with your back to the traffic while you keep walking" routine. You can hear the whoosh of an oncoming car way before it gets close to you. So stop, turn around, and give it one of those looks. They tend to feel sorry for you when you're out in the boondocks. Helps your chances.

If you're tired as hell, forget it. Just stay right there and wait. Somebody will come along sooner or later. Just mind the short hops. If you take a real short one, be sure to LOOK tired.

All of the above assumes you are at least a half-decent judge of distance. If not, start practicing. When you're glommin' down the road in a car, pick something down the road and guess to yourself how far away it is. Then watch the odometer and find out how accurate you were.

If you were off, do it again and adjust your next guess. Stay with it for ten minutes and you'll be an expert. Unless you got serious brain damage or you're blind or something. And don't pick stuff like that mountain range off in the distance in the next state over. Zero in on stuff that's at a distance that'll be useful for deciding whether or not to take a walk. Like a quarter-mile to a couple of miles.

If it's late at night and there's not a soul on the road, we get to go to the next part of this book to talk about what you oughtta do.

The part about sleeping in the great outdoors.

Oh, joy!

Spending The Night Outdoors

Overnighting. Yark! Sleeping in the bushes. Or on the rocks.

Conjures up images of utter destitution and desperation.

Actually though, just like everything else, it's not that way at all. In fact, if you put your brain to work on it, it might even be better than staying home and putting up with a pissed-off wife or girlfriend.

I guess we better start out with a few first principles. Like: Having to overnight never happens when you're thumbing across town or just going a little ways. Think about it. Somebody's BOUND to come by sooner or later when you're near a population center. Which is what you're always gonna be in the middle of when doing local trips. Right? Not only that, but you aren't gonna be all tuckered out from a long days' hitchhiking, either. No need for a nap.

I guess the only time overnighting is even a part of the picture when you're in your own neighborhood is when an opportunity too good to pass up gets dropped in your lap. I confess, I've done it too. Like when you get let out next to a closed gas station at two a.m. with nobody around and they've got some rental camper trailers parked around. Try the door and... alright! It's open. This is illegal as hell, but who's gonna know? You aren't out to trash the place or steal the damn thing, just taking a little snooze. Even if you sleep late and the owner catches you, not much will happen besides a good chewing out. So act real sorry and apologize all over the place and you're on your way. No problem.

So it's cross-country we'll concentrate on, OK? Out in some damn place you never heard of, with zero friends for at least a hundred miles. Whatta you gonna do?

First goddamned thing you're gonna do is: Be dressed for it. It gets cold as hell at night out in the sticks, and you're supposed to already know stuff like this. Go reread the chapter on what the weather can do to you, if you forgot. You're supposed to know the weather can change, too. Don't set out on a long trip thinking that everything's gonna stay just like it is the day you leave. Get a handle on how bad it MIGHT get and then plan on running into just that.

You've also got some kind of duffel bag full of the basic necessities, or a knapsack or something. Right? If not, go back home where it's safe. You don't belong outside.

Have a sheet of plastic in your bundle in case it decides to rain at three a.m. for no good reason. Something that's big enough to cover both the ground and your miserable body at the same time. Sleeping on wet dirt really sucks, and kinda makes going to the trouble of covering your top side look a little dumb, too.

Make sure the fucking basics are taken care before you go worrying about the rest of it.

OK, enough of that. Where you gonna sleep? If you got a lotta time on your hands and ain't in any hurry to arrive somewhere, you might want to ask your latest ride (and if it's getting real late it's probably your last ride whether you like it or not) where the local graveyard is. If you just fetch up somewhere late at night and no cars are on the road, go look for the damn graveyard. Try near a church. Churches get built out in the damnedest boondocks you can imagine. And there's a graveyard next to almost every last one of 'em. Especially out in the country.

If it looks like it might rain, or you just want to get out of the howling gale, skip the graveyard and stay at the church. Get on the lee side under the roof overhang and you'll stay dry. Mostly. And if the cops come by, they take a MUCH kinder view towards those "homeless" folks who've fetched up at the local chapel. You're much less likely to be taken for somebody casing a joint to steal the quarters out of the pinball machines or something.

Back to the graveyard.

As long as it's not pouring or freezing, graveyards are the best places to bed down for the night. Nobody's gonna bother you in a cemetery. And if by chance somebody comes stumbling through the place at half-past midnight, all you have to do is make some noises while remaining out of sight. They won't stick around. Unless they're a cop.

Not only are cemeteries great for being left alone and not getting bothered, they've also got nice soft well-mowed grass to lay your tired body on. Without sandspurs or thistles or poison ivy, either. Plus there's no wild animals. Add lots of out-of-sight places behind headstones and stuff where you can't be seen to be annoyed, and what you've got is the Hilton of the lonesome road.

And the damn things are EVERYWHERE. All over the place. Ain't a town in the country without at least one (and usually a lot more, so as you can pick a nice one) graveyard in it. Plenty of dead people to go around.

Just don't go building a fire to cook your beans on or something. And don't trash the place, either.

When I lived in Hawaii I stayed at a place where this really neat old lady named Myrtle Kaapu (yep, two a's) lived. She put me up in exchange for mowing her gigantic yard (that's the place where the honest-to-God Hawaiian grass shacks were) and carrying heavy stuff for her and all like that.

Anyway, when she was young (back in the 1920s fer chrissakes, can you imagine what the roads must have been like?) she and another girl decided to see America. And they hitchhiked cross country to do it! They each packed a pistol and slept in graveyards (you just KNEW I was gonna get back to the point some fucking time, didn't you?) every place they stayed overnight. Never had a problem. Never had to wave the pistols at anybody, either. But that was back before everybody got so fricking weird from watching TV and the movies.

So if Myrtle could do it forty years before interstate highways, you can sure the hell do it too. Today.

Of course, the world ain't covered over solid with graveyards. Yet. So where else you gonna go?

How 'bout bridges and overpasses? Winos and homeless folks seem to like 'em well enough. You should too. You will definitely meet more folks in places like this than you will in a cemetery. No doubt about it. If you're real gregarious, this is the place for you. The closer to town you get, the likelier it is you'll encounter somebody. Out on the interstate in the depths of Nebraska it's just about as good as a graveyard.

If you spend the night beneath a bridge or someplace similar, pick a good spot under the stupid thing. Don't go lying down where you can get spotted by the cops. They gotta kick your ass out. Even when it's a pain in the ass and they'd rather be doing something else.

Also, try to get into an area as close as possible to where the span connects to the ground. Up where there's not even enough room to stand up without banging your head. Spots like that are much better-protected against the weather. It's hard for the wind to blow rain up in there. That makes it drier. Less windy, and therefore less cold, for that matter, too.

Up in that little crack below the road deck, it's harder to be seen, too. Maybe shove a cardboard box you found in front of you if it's a highway overpass where a cop can shine a light up in there from inside his cruiser. He won't be able to tell if there's really anybody there or not. And he's not very inclined to get out of that nice warm car to go find out as long as nothing's going on.

Abandoned cars are another good spot, too. Once you start looking for them, you'll start seeing 'em all over the place. If it's locked DO NOT do anything stupid like smashing a window to unlock the door. You're smarter than that anyway, though, aren't you? Just keep on going 'till something better comes along.

Don't want to get woke up by a very irate cop or owner while spending the night in a car you vandalized. It's for this reason you also don't want to sack out in one that somebody else smashed either. Might be a teensy bit awkward explaining to everybody's satisfaction that you really didn't do it.

Back to Hawaii. The first time I ever went there I figured I'd just get off the plane and thumb out to the North Shore where the thirty-foot surf is.

Never seen the place in my life before.

Got hung up between Honolulu and Wahiawa. Late at night. And it started pouring rain.

So I said, "Screw this shit!" and jumped into a red Corvair pulled off the road by a construction area. There was a business card on the floor about some kind of kung-fu place.

I didn't really want some joker to give me a karate chop or anything, but since I had no choice I just propped my head on the driver's side arm-rest and fell asleep in the front seat.

Imagine my surprise when, in the middle of the fucking night, the door jerked open and my head fell out and I was staring up at some great big guy who owned the car!

Was it a massacre? Custer's last ride? No. All the guy did was ask me what the hell I was doing there. When I explained what was going on, he just said, "OK," and proceeded to retrieve his car keys from under the seat I'd been sleeping on and left! I went right back to sleep, woke up the next morning, and went on and found the North Shore. The thirty-foot waves weren't there that day, but they did show up later.

That's how easy it is.

I suppose that if I'd trashed the guy's car, things might have been a little different. So be nice, wouldja! You never know when your behavior is gonna get a surprise inspection.

Out where there's nothing for miles and miles, it's a little different, and you just might have to rough it under the stars. If you're stuck, you're stuck. Can't do anything about it.

If that's what it's come down to, don't just go lying on the side of the road. First make damn sure there's no abandoned barns or anything like that out across the field. You might get lucky. Watch out for the varmints, though.

If there's NOTHING around you, go lie on the ground just far enough from the road that no cops or anybody can see you, but not an inch farther. Don't go tramping out through the bushes unless you really have to. Like when it's solid cactus everywhere else or such-all.

The farther from the road you get, the more likely you are to have an unpleasant encounter with a critter or poisonous bug.

And by definition, ANY encounter with a wild animal is unpleasant. You're not gonna sleep worth a shit under the very best of circumstances, and if you get attacked by a swarm of fire ants it'll be a lot worse. Don't go making it any worse than it already is.

You go to sleep on the road shoulder and one of two things is gonna happen: Either some idiot runs you over when he drifts off the pavement, or the cops haul you in. Either way, you lose.

However, roughing it under the stars is a low-probability item. VERY unlikely.

So don't go worrying about sleeping out. You can handle it. And besides, it's great for telling stories about later.

Rush Hour

Rush hour's another charmer. A real winner. In a way, it's kinda like the deal with expressways. Perfect set-up when you first look at it, but then you come to the realization that it sucks. There's sure the hell no lack of cars going by.

People don't stop when they're zooming to or from work. There IS a slight tendency for things to be better in the morning instead of the afternoon, but not much. I dunno, I guess they're all just barely gonna make it on time, or maybe they're already late, and the half a minute it takes to stop for you is more than they can deal with. Or maybe they're all pissed off cause the boss shit on 'em, and they hate everything and everybody. Who the hell knows?

Since people are much less inclined to slow down and stop, you might want to get over to that intersection where they all gotta stop. Maybe do the routine from in front of the intersection like I described earlier. Just be sure you're someplace where they go past you at minimum speed.

Really, though, there's not much you can do about rush hour. If traffic's heavy and they're all doing Mach three, you might be better off forgetting it for a while. Go have a burger somewhere and wait for things to ease back.

Keep track of the time right, and you won't have to fuck with it. Just hitchhike some other time.

Commuting To And From Work

OK, now that I've just finished telling you you can't thumb during rush hour, I'm gonna talk about something that forces you to be out on the road at that exact time.

Nice of me, huh?

Hitchhiking to work and back. Piece of cake if you know what you're doing. Most of what you're doing consists of all that tangental shit I already told you about, like your appearance and what you do AFTER you get picked up. The need for a good appearance is obvious. During rush hour there's gonna be a lot more "normal"-type people on the road, and a whole lot less other folks. "Normal" people don't go in for giving rides to raggly-looking guys out on the side of the road.

Not to worry, though, because since you're headed to the job you already got the right clothes on. You're dressed for success.

Or something.

So forget appearance. You already look just fine. Let's talk about the rest, then. Way back in the beginning of this book somewhere, I told you all about extending a ride through your behavior AFTER you were in the car and humming down the road.

Well, here's another reason to have your shit together when inside someone's car.

Repeat business.

That's right, repeat rides from the same people. If you do it right, the same folks give you the same rides, from the same corners, at the same times, every day. Neat, huh?

Since you gotta be somewhere at the same time every day, people (who also just happen to have to be somewhere at the same time every day) are gonna see you day after day. Sooner or later, they won't be able to stand it and will stop and pick you up if for no other reason than to find out what the hell you're doing out there all the time.

And that's when you got 'em. Once they discover you're just a little guy fighting a big world to make a success of yourself by having to hitchhike twenty miles a day to hold down a job, they're hooked. So long as you don't fuck up a good thing by being an asshole, that is.

People admire somebody who's fighting heavy odds to better himself. You fit the bill exactly when you're out there day after day ON YOUR WAY TO WORK.

"What a guy! I admire that in a guy."

Just don't tell 'em it's not as bad as they think it is.

After a couple of weeks of daily hitchhiking to work, you're basically home free. The very same people will stop for you every fucking day. Like clockwork. If you fuck up and somebody comes along and picks you up BEFORE your usual guy comes by, you can almost take a break and not hitchhike at all at that next corner until it's time for that NEXT usual guy to come along.

Although it IS slower than driving to work yourself, hitchhiking to work has one definite advantage over using your own car. You never gotta worry about breakdowns. Or running out of gas. Or flat tires. Or anything.

After you've been commuting for a while and you've developed a group of regulars who you can depend on to pick you up (and there's gonna be more than one for each of the places/times you will be frequenting), you'll find that car problems just go away and disappear. Weird but true. SOMEBODY will ALWAYS be along. And if their car breaks down, guess what? You just walk over to the edge of the pavement and get the hell out of there.

But be sure to ask them if there's anything you can do for them before you leave.

If you ever want them to give you another ride.

Pretty cool, huh?

Cross-Country

Cross-country hitchhiking is a real giggle. What a way to see the whole U.S.A.! You can go any damn place you feel like.

Give yourself a month or three in the summer and GO! Maybe stop somewhere for a while and get some kind of job every so often to keep you in food. Since you have zero expenses, a minimum-wage job (never mind what a carpenter's wage or something like that brings) will be more than you can spend.

Work a week and play for three. Or whatever you feel like.

When you're covering large distances and getting those loooong rides to whothehellknowswhere, you have plenty of time to really get to know whoever it is that's giving you the ride. Often as not, they'll tell you all about places to go, places to avoid, places and people to see about jobs and a whole world of other stuff. There's no better perspective on a place than the one that somebody who already lives there has.

You think you're on your way to Crater Lake in Oregon (a truly spectacular place), and after talking to somebody for five hundred miles of Texas highway you suddenly find yourself agreeing to spend a couple of weeks on his farm in Montana helping him with the cattle. Maybe he'll teach you to pan for gold or something. No telling.

That's half the fun of cross-country. Sudden changes in the plan. Just for the hell of it.

America is a BIG place and there's so much stuff out there you'll NEVER get to do it all. And there's stuff out there you never imagined. People doing things you wouldn't have believed unless you saw and did it yourself.

So go. And have fun. But if you're gonna do it, do it right. Better bring some stuff along with you. BUT DON'T BRING ANYTHING FANCY THAT MIGHT MAKE SOME ASSHOLE WANT TO STEAL IT. Take things you can sleep outside in. Stuff you don't mind if it gets soaked through in a surprise thunderstorm.

And travel LIGHT.

After you've packed your rucksack or bag or whatever (I went from Florida to California carrying everything I owned in the world packed inside a laundry bag once), go back and take a third of it out and stash it somewhere or just give it to somebody. YOU DON'T NEED ALL THAT SHIT. Some jeans, shirts, a coat, toothbrush, shoes, what else is there?

If you're SURE you aren't gonna wind up in West Yellowstone or the mountains of Vermont or some kind of place like that, you don't even need the coat. If you can just lie on the ground and still get enough sleep to do you, then ditch the blanket. Don't mind being soaked? Forget the sheet of plastic. And if, out there in the wilderness, you change your mind, no sweat. Pick it up CHEAP at the Salvation Army thrift store. Or some church sale. Ask the guy who's giving you the ride. He knows where all that stuff is.

138

How easy can it be? You'll meet the neatest people, see the prettiest places and do the damnedest things.

What are you waiting for?

Giving Other Hitchhikers Rides When It's You That's Driving

OK, it won't be long now. You're almost finished with this thing.

In fact, this last part isn't even about hitchhiking. No.

It's about GIVING rides. Not getting 'em. So you're already an expert. How 'bout that? But don't throw this down and rush outside for the highway.

Not yet.

You need to know how to give people rides when it comes your turn to do it. And one of the first things that happens to people who start hitchhiking is that they feel obligated to pick up their fellow travelers by the roadside when they get behind the wheel themselves. You develop a fine appreciation of what all those guys out on the side of the road are going through.

So let's do it right, OK?

If you've been paying more than... oh, say half-attention to what I've been going on and about with in here, you already probably have a pretty good idea of how to go about giving rides to hitchhikers. That's right, only pick up the same kind of hitchhikers that I've been trying to turn you into.

And that's not just because I want all those other guys to get pissed off 'cause nobody's picking 'em up and force 'em to have to go out and buy this. Not at all. Well... maybe just a little. Never mind.

Think about it. Who do you want in your car? Some scumbucket or a normal person? Leave the scumbuckets to their fellow dregs.

There's enough of 'em out there to make sure the guy gets where he's going. And don't go feeling guilty about it. Some of these jokers got the crabs, or scabies, or worse. Stuff you don't gotta go to bed with 'em to get. Stuff that jumps off 'em and strolls on over to greener pastures (that's you). How you gonna convince your girlfriend you got the crabs (and then proceeded to give them to her as a special gift) from a hitchhiker? Sure fucking thing!

It's just like getting INSIDE the car. YOU, and nobody else, are in control. Use your eyes. Or eye.

Something to keep in mind is what kind of place the guy's thumbing at. Is there an obstruction that would prevent you from seeing his buddy with the knife in his hand? For that matter, what kind of neighborhood is it? Is it the kind of place you wouldn't feel comfortable walking around in? All this stuff's trying to tell you something. Listen.

If it's a girl thumbing, does she look like a whore? If she does (and you're smart enough to want to stay the hell away from prostitutes) then keep on driving. Sometimes guys will hide in the bushes or around the corner and let their girl be the piece of bait

140

(remember way back when when I mentioned PEOPLE as props?) to
pull victims in. Does it look like one of those deals?

It's OK to judge a book by its cover in this situation.
Got the idea?
Enough of that shit. You should have an eye for that kind of stuff.

How 'bout pulling off the road to pick the poor shlub up? Is there
a ditch? A curb? Nothing, so you gotta stop everybody while you stay
in the traffic lane? Soft sand that you'll get bogged down in up to your
doorhandles?

Play it safe. NEVER NEVER NEVER stop right out there on the
pavement. Even if there's nobody behind you. If a cop doesn't come
whamming out of the bushes, a car you never saw will come
whamming up your asshole.

Don't go slamming brakes, either. One time I watched a guy go
around some fuckhead driving a red convertible Thunderbird who had
stopped suddenly for me. He went around us sideways with rubber
smoking on all four tires. He didn't lose it and go into the palmettos or
hit anybody in the oncoming lane.

And he didn't come back and shoot us either. But he should have.

Has the guy hitchhiking decided to set up shop in the middle of a
curve where nobody's gonna see you've stopped 'till it's too late?

Is there room to get up to speed before merging into the traffic? Is there so damn much traffic you'll never get back on the road at any speed?

Any cops around who might decide to bust you for an unsafe lane change?

And on and on and on...

Stay safe. Stay legal.
I'm tired. Let's go get a beer.

YOU WILL ALSO WANT TO READ: